Tom Slemen
# HAUNTED
# WIRRAL

For Pat Woodward and Addy Walker

Edited by Claire Walker
Published by The Bluecoat Press, Liverpool
Book design by March Design, Liverpool
Printed by The Universities Press

ISBN 1872568 93 9

Tom Slemen
# HAUNTED
## WIRRAL

The Bluecoat Press

# Contents

## Spiritual Encounters

## The Bizarre and the Unexplained

## Creepy Coincidences

## Hauntings

# Introduction

As I write the introduction to this book, not with a word processor, but with a biro and notebook on my knee, under a very untypical azure sky, I am sitting on a bench at the Pier Head on the Liverpool side of the River Mersey, contemplating the peninsula of Wirral. To my right, I can vaguely see the morning mist-shrouded waterfronts of Seacombe, Egremont and New Brighton – once the exotic destinations of many a child, before the dawn of cheap air travel. Straight ahead, past the Mersey-skimming gulls, I can see Birkenhead, where ferries have been plying to and fro since 1330, when Edward II granted a charter establishing the original ferry over the River Mersey from the Birkenhead Priory. Could the monks who crossed the Mersey in those times have dreamt that ships to rival Noah's Ark, would one day be built on those shores in the mammoth shipyards of Cammel Laird, where many of the military Leviathans which saved our necks in two world wars were constructed and launched?

Then my gaze falls on Port Sunlight Village, created by the social visionary, William Hesketh Lever, in 1889. Hesketh Lever came looking for a place to build a soap works, but hit on the novel idea of not only building a factory, but of also building local houses for his workforce. At a price of £200 per acre, he bought 56 acres of land and set about creating his dream of a small-scale Utopia. All of this local history is just one aspect of Wirral, and what I have mentioned so far is just the stuff of any local history book.

The Wirral which I have been concerned with is a peninsula of ghosts, phantoms, spectres, doppelgangers, premonitions, reincarnations, astral voyages to another world and timeslips. The cases in *Haunted Wirral* confirm the old adage that truth really is stranger than fiction. I had assumed that a book on Wirral ghosts would include the same old weathered yarns about Mother Redcap's ghost and the spectres of smugglers, but the mysterious peninsula proved to be a stranger place than even I took it to be, with tales weirder than anything found within the books of Stephen King, or Rod Serling's *Twilight Zone*. Take the intriguing case of the girl born to Wirral parents who became so infatuated with a long-dead crusader, that she ended up being whisked back in time to the 14th century to become his fiancée. There are the ghostly tales about a haunted wardrobe, which is still out there and could be in your bedroom; a black obsidian mirror, which allows unwise dabblers into the occult to summon forth any dead person, and the dead man who turned up at a school reunion in Leasowe.

I touch on the subject of reincarnation in this book, and whenever I think of the concept of rebirth, I always recall an incident that happens to have a Wirral link. In 2001, I came to Ellesmere Port for a book-signing at Borders bookshop in Cheshire Oaks. After the signing, and an impromptu talk on the subject of ghosts, a large, thickset man named John Helsby came up to me and said he knew for certain that he had been born before. A few people present were apparently amused by the man's extreme claim, but I was prepared to listen to what he had to say. John explained to me that since he was a child, he could vividly remember Viking longboats bringing him ashore to fight pitched battles with the natives of the country he was invading. John described an intrinsic love he had for Scandinavian folklore tales about Valhalla, Thor, Odin, Loki, Asgard and so on. I suggested that to unravel the mystery he should either visit a hypnotist, so he could possibly be regressed, or learn how to explore his own past life through the technique of auto-suggestion. The latter basically involves going back through the events of the day in your mind as you lie in bed. You then travel back mentally through the events of a week and so on, until you have enough cerebral muscle power to take your mind back entire years. It isn't important how far you go back initially; what is important is the directing of the mind in a backward, retrograde direction, because once you fall asleep, your subconscious mind will continue to dredge the past and may create dreams from incidents from a period beyond the past of your current lifetime.

In a novel entitled *Altered States* (released as a film in 1981) the author, Paddy Chayefsky, argued that our evolutionary past is encoded in our genetic make-up. In the novel and the film, the hero uses sensory deprivation techniques and psychotropic drugs to relive his past incarnations as a primitive, hairy hominid, and even as a primordial organic puddle.

Some may think that *Altered States* is pure bunkum, but in 2002, the beginnings of a genetic survey of Wirral was carried out by scientists at the University of Nottingham and University College, London. The object of the unusual survey was to find the genetic code of Vikings who settled in Wirral in 902 AD. That year, the Vikings, initially led by the Norwegian Viking, Ingimund, spread throughout the Wirral peninsula as far as south Chester and across the Mersey to populate South West Lancashire. The results of the genetic survey proved, beyond a doubt, that a high proportion of the Wirral population has Viking blood in their veins. The scientists who carried out the survey asked volunteers with specific names derived from Scandinavian surnames to provide DNA samples via mouth swabs. One surname that is certainly derived from a Viking name is Helsby – the surname of John Helsby, the man who told me that he believed he had been born before as a Viking marauder.

Whether you are a descendant of a Viking, a Norman, a Celt, an Anglo-Saxon, or possibly a Neanderthal, I hope you'll enjoy the weird and fascinating stories on the following pages.


Tom Slemen

# Ghostly Visions

## A Little Girl's Advice

In August 2000, Ray Sinclair of Dovecot received a sizeable legacy upon the death of his Aunt Frieda in Wales. The amount bequeathed to Ray enabled him to purchase a grand Edwardian house for his family in the Egremont area of Wirral. The Sinclairs had three children: two sons, aged 19 and 21, who had left home, and a ten-year-old daughter named Brittany.

Brittany loved the new house. It had a sprawling back garden to play in, and was quite close to the waterfront. The young girl was adored by her parents, and when she became infatuated with the airy top-floor front room, they said it could be hers. Under Brittany's close direction, her father painted the bedroom walls candy pink, and had the entire wooden floor polished; nothing was too good for his little girl.

It was while the room was being so prettily decorated, that a strange thing occurred – Mr Sinclair opened wide the windows of the room and left the door ajar slightly to allow the paint to dry faster. With the bulk of the job completed, he turned off the light and wearily made his way to bed. The house was silent, as his wife and little girl were already sleeping. Once his head hit the pillow, his eyes felt heavy and he was drifting into a deep, peaceful sleep, when he heard a distinctly loud click. He quickly jumped out of bed and on to the landing. To his confusion, he saw that the light was back on in the room he had just been decorating. Confused, he looked into the bare room, and switched the light back off.

However, the following morning, Ray noticed that the light was again burning in that room, and seemed to have been on for a considerable time. He knew that no one else was up and so nobody had been in there before him. This, along with a few other unusual but trivial occurrences, made Ray mildly suspect that perhaps his new house could be haunted. However, not wishing to upset his wife or daughter, he did not voice his fears. But, erring on the side of caution, Ray had the wiring checked. A qualified electrician assured him, after a thorough inspection, that there was nothing amiss in Brittany's new bedroom, or the rest of the house.

On the very first night that Ray put his daughter to bed in that new room, as he ruffled her hair affectionately, he experienced a feeling of intense anxiety. He hoped that the light bulb incident had just been some figment of his overtired imagination. He sat on Brittany's bed with a book open on his lap, but instead of telling her a story, he asked her to sing a new song that she had learnt.

Brittany's latest ambition was to be a famous singer. Her face exploded into a beaming smile, and she started to sing a song by the pop group, Steps. Three songs later, Brittany's eyelids started to flicker, and her head started to nod as she became sleepy. Ray leant over and kissed his daughter softly on her forehead. He switched off the bedside lamp, then tiptoed out of the room.

Ray got into bed and was just snuggling into the covers next to his wife, when a child's scream pierced the silence. It was Brittany. Ray hurled himself out of bed and yanked open the bedroom door. He dashed across the landing and barged into his daughter's room. Brittany was just a silhouette of a bundle, shivering under her covers. As she cried on her father's shoulder, she told him that "an old man in old clothes" had appeared in her room and had switched on the light. He had then whispered to her: "Please leave the light on, I'm afraid of the dark," before vanishing right before her eyes.

Brittany was terrified and slept between her parents that night. On the following night, her mother convinced her that she had imagined the strange man and had only suffered a nightmare but Ray Sinclair felt uncomfortable about the whole episode. He suspected that the ghostly man had been real, but said nothing. That night, Brittany was helped into bed and reassured that nothing else would wake her up. Yet, this time000000 within moments, her bedroom windows flew open. An aged man with a wild-looking head of silver hair and staring blue eyes appeared. This time, Brittany didn't scream out for help. She was instead very calm and bravely asked the elusive figure: "Who are you?"

The ghost, for that was what he was, sat himself down on her bed. He explained to her that his name was Ernest and that he had died in her room a long time ago, and that moments before he died, everything had gone dark. He shuddered as he explained to her that he had asked those at his deathbed to open the curtains to admit more light, but instead they had let him pass away in the darkness. Ernest explained that he was terrified of the dark, because it was so like the blackness in his coffin. Brittany clutched her Tellytubby doll, engrossed by his spooky explanations. She looked up at the man. Smiling with her eyes wide and hopeful, she suggested that Ernest should go and see God if he was scared. The old man bowed his head, and in a broken voice, he confessed to her that he had done something very wrong once, and was afraid to meet his Maker as a result. Brittany continued to smile, not understanding his concern.

"Don't worry, Ernest," she said, innocently, "if you're really sorry about what you did, God will still love you."

The apparition seemed to give a lot of thought to the girl's seemingly naive words. He stood up awkwardly and shuffled towards the window, before turning back to look at her.

"You're a lovely lassie. A little angel," he said.

He looked up and smiled, then faded clean away, right before her eyes. The ghost was never seen again after that night, and the light in Brittany's room never switched itself on again.

I was intrigued by the unusual ghostly tale, and decided to conduct some research into the history of the building. I discovered that an Ernest Mossop did indeed once live at the Egremont house, where he remained until his death around 1910, but I have been unable to establish  whether or not his ghost was the troubled shade who took a little girl's good advice.

# Meeting by Starlight

Although the following incident didn't take place in Wirral, I've included it because the two witnesses involved in the case were from Heswall.

In 1978, in Liverpool, there was a club located at the bottom of Mount Pleasant and Brownlow Hill called the Hofbrauhaus. The theme and layout of the club was that of a German bier keller. At the Hofbrauhaus, in June 1978, a hen party was held for a girl named June. Two of the guests, Dawn and Sandra, both aged 26, and both graduates of Liverpool University, were very good friends who lived next door to each other in a lane off Telegraph Road, Heswall.

During the hen party, as the wine and conversation flowed freely, Dawn and Sandra began to discuss how it seemed that all their friends were either getting married, or settling down into nine-to-five jobs. Becoming more determined about their own fate as the night wore on, the two feisty girls made a drunken pact not to let themselves be forced into the rat race. They had no intention of settling down. Dawn then suggested that the two of them should embark upon a backpacking trek across France, and later in the year, they could even travel across America. Dawn and Sandra clinked a toast to their new resolution of staying footloose and free.

In the following month of July, Dawn and Sandra began their journey across France, starting in the countryside of Picardie, where they pitched a tent and enjoyed the glorious sunshine. Days later they moved on to Auvers, a small town in the countryside north of Paris. They set up their tent in a secluded area on the outskirts of town, overlooking vast wheatfields. The date was Wednesday 26 July 1978. Dawn wore a wristwatch that displayed the date and the day of the week on the dial, and she could clearly see that it read 'Wednesday'. As the twilight gathered, the girls opened a celebratory bottle of wine which they had purchased earlier that day while passing through the quiet town.

Sipping the wine, they watched the stars come out in the open sky above the fields. Everything was so tranquil, and Dawn and Sandra sighed as a bright shooting star seemed to fall to earth. "Make a wish!" they yelled out in unison, exploding into giggles. Away from all the artificial lighting that blots out the stars in the cities, the sky above Dawn and Sandra was so bright with starlight and the mystical glow of the Milky Way, that they could see the surrounding wheatfields quite clearly. There was something almost magical about the beauty of the evening.

However, the mood soon turned sour. Just after midnight, something very bizarre took place. Dawn glanced at the luminous dial of her watch, fully expecting Thursday to appear in the day of the week window on the dial, but instead it clearly displayed Sunday. She leant over and showed Sandra, who agreed that the watch was reading the incorrect day and was equally confused.

"Look!" Sandra suddenly exclaimed, pointing to a figure quickly approaching from across the field.

The figure was holding what appeared to be a shield and a sword. Unsure of the intentions of the approaching stranger, they nipped away and hid behind the tent, and Dawn grabbed the wine bottle, ready to hit the odd-looking stranger, should he come too close.

In the starlight, as he neared them, the girls got a better view of the man. In actual fact he wasn't holding a sword and a shield at all. He was actually clutching a large piece of canvas on an easel, and he was carrying some type of brush holder in the other hand. They could not make out any detail of his face.

As the girls stared on curiously, they saw the man suddenly drop to his knees about fifty yards away from them. He started screaming, before throwing down the canvas and the brushes, which landed near Dawn and Sandra.

Sandra immediately felt sorry for the man. Perhaps it was the wine encouraging irrational sentimentality, but she thought he looked like a typical tormented artistic genius. She stood up and started walking towards him, full of empathy. Dawn was far from sympathetic.

"Sandra, don't!" she called out, but her friend continued walking out from the shadows of the tent.

The man was lying prostrate on the ground, sobbing, with his head buried in his hands. Dawn followed Sandra over to the distressed artist. She could speak several languages, and in French she casually tried to greet the man. Hearing her voice, he slowly raised his head to look up at her. His bearded face looked pale, and his eyes revealed some deep inner torment. He seemed haunted. He scrambled to his feet, and while doing so, reached into a pocket in his jacket – producing a revolver! The girls froze in sheer terror at the sight of the weapon. The man began to mutter something which Sandra was unable to understand, but Dawn recognised the Dutch tones and began to carefully back away, pulling Sandra hard as she did so.

Dawn initiated a brief conversation in Dutch with the man. Unable to understand, Sandra felt uncomfortable and began to feel weak at the knees as the agitated man kept gazing back at the revolver in his hand. He said something to Dawn which made her nod slowly, before she then turned her back on him and walked away, roughly pushing Sandra ahead of her.

"I don't want to die," stammered Sandra, fearing the worst, expecting to be shot in the back at any second.

Although she was afraid, she could not resist the urge to look back at the man, and as she did so, she saw something that was to haunt her for the rest of her life. There stood the artist, motionless, staring up at the sky with tears streaming down his face, pointing the barrel of the revolver towards his chest. Then, there was a flash of light and a loud crack, and the man fell backwards, his body continuing to flinch for some moments after the fall. Dawn and Sandra ran over to see if they could help him in any way, but he waved them away with his gun, before unsteadily rising to his feet. Blood was bubbling out of the hole in his chest, yet he managed to stagger away across the field.

Dawn and Sandra were in complete shock and ran pell-mell all the way to a distant farmhouse. Passing through the rickety gate to the premises, they encountered an angry dog, followed by a disgruntled farmer. On seeing the man, the girls exploded with words, as they tried to explain what had just happened to them. In a state of panic, they insisted that he call the police immediately. When the farmer calmed them down and asked them to explain what they had just experienced, he visibly paled at their awful story. Without speaking, he led the girls into the farmhouse and sat them down. After a lengthy pause, he sighed, shivered, and explained to them that they had just encountered a ghost.

Apparently, the ghost had been seen many times at that specific time of year. It was believed to be the apparition of Vincent Van Gogh, who shot himself in that very field on Sunday 27 July 1890. Other people claimed to have seen the pathetic looking ghost heading towards the old inn where Van Gogh had staggered after he had shot himself. Vincent had died in his brother's arms there a few days later. This naturally sent shivers down the girls' spines, and that night they swiftly rolled up the tent and left the area. Sandra and Dawn still live in Heswall, and they often talk about the unbelievable night when they met the tortured shade of Vincent Van Gogh.

## The Roaming Corpse

A lot of people ask me whether there is any particular story relating to the occult that scares me. The story that I am about to relate – which I have researched for many years now – certainly unsettles me, because it's about a power which should be withheld from the human race for the time being: the power to raise the dead.

In the late 1980s, shortly after the Berlin Wall came down, sinister video footage was smuggled out of the crumbling Soviet Union. It showed a man with alleged psychic powers apparently reviving a corpse. I remember the scene clearly; the psychic's face was out of shot, but his hands were visible, and they waved in the air across the badly smashed-up corpse of a car crash victim, on a mortuary slab. The corpse lifted its left arm, apparently in response to the commands of the eerie 'miracle worker'. What became of the 'resurrection man' is unknown, but it is known that the former Soviet Union poured a lot of money into psychical research, particularly into healing and tissue regeneration by paranormal means.

The idea of raising the dead may seem morbidly distasteful, but the Bible records that Jesus, his disciples Peter and Paul, and the prophets Elijah and Elisha, also raised the dead. The most famous account of reviving a corpse is when Jesus raised Lazarus. Then there are the mysterious words which Jesus uttered – "Talitha, cumi," – when he brought the deceased daughter of Jairius back to life. It has been speculated that the two words which Christ spoke, when translated, mean: "Little girl, I say to you, arise."

For centuries, occultists of the highest order have claimed that there is a supernatural way to bring back the dead, but only for a limited period. These claims may seem outlandish, but there are well-documented stories of so-called Necromancers – black magicians who revive recently buried corpses to quiz them for information – being at large across England, including Merseyside.

In the 1970s, Nathaniel, an accomplished master of the Black Arts from Wallasey, attended the funeral of his 75-year-old uncle in the Mossley Hill district of Liverpool. The body of his uncle – a Mr James – was put in an open coffin in the front parlour, and family and friends all paid their respects. Mrs James searched the house from top to bottom to find the secret savings her late husband was known to have hidden, but she couldn't find the nest egg anywhere.

On the night before the funeral, at 8.45pm, Mrs James returned from her neighbour's to find the door of the front parlour locked. She looked into the room through the bay window and was horrified to see that the coffin was empty. In a state of shock she walked to the nearby police station and reported the bizarre incident, but when she returned, she found that the parlour was now unlocked and the corpse was back in its coffin.

On the following day, Nathaniel produced a bundle of money, and claimed it was the savings which Mr James had hidden. The money had been hidden under the grate of the boarded-up fireplace in the back room. Nathaniel would not reveal how he had located the hidden money, but his cousin later provided a spine-chilling explanation, and his story was backed up by three independent witnesses. He claimed that Nathaniel had used black magic to bring Mr James back to life so that he could ask him where the money was. Amazingly, the pallid, rigid corpse had stirred in its coffin. After a moment of tense anticipation, the impressed onlookers were stunned when, in a slurred voice, the corpse revealed the exact whereabouts of his savings.

Creepier still, as Nathaniel and his cousin hurried to find the money hidden in the back room, Mr James actually rose up and left his coffin. The deceased man apparently then took himself off on a walkabout, visiting his old local pub – where he was allegedly seen by three terrified drinkers, who could not believe their eyes. Then, the zombie-like corpse was taken via a taxi-cab back to the house on Mossley Hill and had climbed back into his coffin, before Mrs James returned with the police. On the following day, the wandering corpse was laid to rest, and hopefully that is where it will remain – that is until Judgement Day, when the dead will all supposedly rise again.

In the late 1970s, the *Liverpool Echo* reported that a Wirral man and two accomplices had been arrested in a Birkenhead cemetery whilst trying to exhume the grave of a recently-buried friend. The three men said they had intended to revive the corpse through the use of Black Magic. One of the three would-be resurrection men was none other than Nathaniel, the occultist who allegedly revived the body of his uncle in Mossley Hill. What is even more spine-chilling, is that Nathaniel is still said to be at large in Wirral …

# House Call

At exactly nine o'clock on the evening of Friday 20 March 1887, Duncan Alexander, a 50-year-old doctor, hastened from his Birkenhead surgery, carrying his Gladstone bag and clutching his hat in the fierce out-of-season gales which had just blown the Ferry Landing Stage out into the Mersey. Dr Alexander followed 13-year-old Obadiah Walker towards his nearby Conway Street home, where his young sister Martha was in a semi-conscious state after choking on a boiled sweet. Young Obadiah kept stopping, and turning to the physician, urging him to hurry to the aid of his beloved six-year-old sister.

Unknown to Obadiah, Duncan Alexander was a man with a serious addiction problem; he was an alcoholic, and whenever he encountered the slightest degree of stress, or whenever he came under the slightest amount of pressure, he sought refuge in a bottle of gin. Tonight, the doctor knew he would have to perform a tracheotomy – a delicate incision into the choking child's windpipe to allow air into her bursting, oxygen-starved lungs. Already his hands were trembling. The delirium tremens was upon him. With his body tremoring, his mouth started to dry up, and a sickening dizziness overwhelmed him. As he strode along after the anxious boy, the yellow lights of the street lamps seemed to dance about before his gaze. Practically convulsing, the distracted doctor turned a corner and became transfixed by the sight of a nearby public house. The shadows of the drinkers against the frosted window panes and the faint hubbub of singing and laughter gripped his fevered mind. Like a moth to a flame, the pub lamps drew him in, and he suddenly announced to Obadiah, "Run ahead and inform your mother that I'll be along shortly. I have to see the landlord in here, but I shan't be very long."

Obadiah returned a puzzled grimace, but before he could question the doctor, Duncan Alexander had slipped into the public house. The boy ran homeward through the blustery night and told his mother, Mrs Lydia Walker, who was waiting anxiously for their return. She was outraged by the doctor's detour into the pub, but dared not leave her sick daughter unattended.

It was not until half-past nine that Dr Alexander hammered on the door of the Conway Street house, and was greeted with a rain of blows from an hysterical Mrs Walker. Her little girl Martha was dead. He was too late to save her. Nevertheless, Dr Alexander queasily pushed past the distraught woman. He looked up and saw Obadiah standing on the stairs in tears, and so he rushed up to the bedroom where he found little Martha, lying cold and blue on the bed. The doctor desperately tried smelling salts and every trick in his medical repertoire, but the little girl couldn't be revived.

Not long after the tragic loss, the doctor was found dead at the bottom of the staircase at his home, after stumbling down the stairs in a drunken haze.

It was a year after his unexpected death that a stranger knocked at the house in Conway Street at 9.30pm. Lydia Walker's sister Phoebe answered – and was faced with a sad-looking man standing on the doorstep, wearing a Homburg hat and a cape. He carried a doctor's bag.

"Dr Alexander," he announced, and rushed past Phoebe into the house.

He quickly made his way up the stairs in silence, but when Phoebe chased after the stranger, she found the rooms upstairs empty. Naturally concerned, the girl soon related the strange incident to Lydia, who shuddered when she heard the doctor's name. The unknown visitor had obviously been the restless ghost of the guilt-ridden, late Dr Alexander.

But the unusual occurrences did not end there.

One sweltering evening in May 1976, a 12-year-old girl named Amanda was put to bed. She lived at the exact same house in Conway Street that had once been inhabited by the Walker family. At around 9.30pm, Amanda was startled to see an old fashioned man come into her room. He wore what she described as a "funny black hat and a cloak" – and clutched an old leather bag. He took off his coat, and went to the bathroom along the landing to fetch a bowl of water and a flannel. He dabbed Amanda's forehead and used a long-handled spoon to administer a purple, sweet-tasting medicine from a bottle. The girl assumed he was some modern – but eccentric – doctor, that her mother must have called. The physician smiled benevolently and seemed to have tears in his eyes as he gently bade her goodnight.

That morning at one o'clock, Amanda rose from her sickbed with a sudden ravenous appetite and went down to the kitchen to raid the fridge. Her feverish sickness had completely gone. Her parents were alarmed by her explanation about the doctor, for they had not called out any doctor. Immediately they searched the house – but the mysterious doctor could not be found.

A month afterwards, an elderly neighbour told them the sad story about the alcoholic doctor, and how his restless guilty shade called at the house each May, forever trying to save the little girl he had let down so badly. In the following May the ghost failed to call, so we must assume that he is now at peace.


## Reaper at the Roadside

The rainy Sunday night of 12 August will remain embedded in the memory of a certain retired bricklayer named Gene until his dying day. Upon that Sunday, at ten minutes to twelve, Gene swiftly drank his last vodka and tonic and left a public house in the district of Thingwall. He walked unsteadily through heavy rain to his Ford Cortina in the pub carpark, a little the worse for drink. He'd been drinking with friends at the pub since 7pm, and now, dangerously over the limit, he was to embark on the journey home to Noctorum.

After stalling the vehicle as he was leaving the carpark, Gene switched on the car radio, which was tuned to Radio City. As the booming tone of the radio presenter's voice echoed around the empty carpark, he quickly restarted the engine and was soon travelling up Barnston Road. Not only was he drunk, Gene was also speeding along as the rain lashed down. Suddenly, he noticed a man in black standing at the roadside, about two hundred yards up ahead of him. The figure looked like a policeman to Gene, so he slowed down and quickly turned down the volume on the radio. The car neared the silhouetted figure, and Gene was able to see that the person standing at the roadside was a black man, dressed in a black suit and a black polo neck sweater. He raised his arm as Gene's Cortina approached. The high intake of alcohol had made him feel quite charitable, and he did what he normally would never have done when sober – he stopped for a hitchhiker.

Before Gene could even lean over to unlock the passenger door, the man in black had entered the vehicle, yet he was certain that the passenger door had been locked. The stranger slammed shut the car door and relaxed back into his seat.

"Where do you want to go?" Gene inquired, with a slight slur in his voice.

"The roundabout, up ahead," the stranger answered, speaking in a low voice, without even turning to face the driver.

Gene clumsily fumbled with the clutch control, and as the Cortina shuddered and moved off, the man announced: "I have to pick a child up as well."

"You what?" Gene muttered, confused.

"I'm Death!"

The man turned at last to face Gene.

Gene realised that he had foolishly let a stranger into his vehicle, and that, worse still, he had obviously picked up a man with a serious mental problem. Gene immediately started to think of ways to get rid of his deluded passenger, who was beginning to make him feel very uncomfortable.

"You die tonight, Gene," he said. "And you kill a child at this roundabout."

Gene was more than uncomfortable by this stage and desperately wanted to let the man out. He attempted to brake, but the car refused to stop. The gear stick was somehow locked in position, as was the steering wheel, which refused to turn, even a fraction of an inch. Gene swore, fear and panic rising up inside him, as he kept trying to stop the vehicle. No matter what Gene tried, the speedometer stayed at a steady 55 miles per hour. He took his foot off the accelerator pedal completely, but the car continued to speed along, heading straight towards a junction. Beyond that was the long stretch of Arrowe Park Road – then the roundabout. Beads of sweat formed on Gene's face and forehead, and an icy chill coursed through his body. It all felt like a nightmare, but one in which the dreamer cannot wake. He contemplated jumping from the vehicle and tried the door handle, but like the steering wheel, it refused to budge.

What unsettled Gene even more, was the car radio, which, instead of playing pop music, was now emitting funereal organ music. Worse still, before him in the windscreen of the doomed Cortina, Gene could clearly see the faint images of two coffins materialising. One of the coffins was small, and Gene understood that it must be that of the child he was about to kill in the accident. With terror gripping his heart, he let go of the wheel and turned to the man who was undoubtedly the Grim Reaper himself, and pleaded for mercy.

"What about my children? My wife and kids?" sobbed Gene, verging on hysteria.

But his desperate words fell upon deaf ears. Not a trace of mercy could be detected in the poker-faced personification of death, who simply replied:

"At the back of your mind you knew this would happen. You knew that drinking and getting behind the wheel of a car would come to this one day, so you obviously think nothing of the people you are going to leave behind."

"Please, I'll do anything," Gene begged, staring in dread through the swaying windscreen wipers at the dark and dismal road ahead. The ghostly coffins then appeared to melt away to reveal the crying face of a distressed little girl. Gene's insides churned over. It was the face of his own, darling, seven-year-old daughter, Emily.

"When you die, your wife gradually gets over it, and she marries again. The man she marries ends up beating her, and also abuses Emily. Emily starts drinking, and she also ends up as an alcoholic."

The blunt delivery of such an awful scenario tormented Gene to thbreaking point.

"Please, let me have another chance," he cried.

The Grim Reaper said nothing and Gene suddenly felt resigned to the terrible fate ahead of him.

"Is there an after-life?" he asked, his voice quivering.

Again, his question was not answered. The cruel silence was almost palpable. Then, as the Cortina sped past the grand gates of Landican Cemetery, the sinister passenger suddenly spoke.

"Here it comes," he said.

Up ahead, Gene could make out several cars which were proceeding round the roundabout and heading to various exits. He could clearly see a Give Way line on the road ahead, but still he was unable to stop the car. As it hurtled towards the roundabout, out of control, three boys suddenly ran out of a field opposite and raced across the road. The last boy was just not quick enough, and in a second he was caught squarely in the headlights of the speeding Cortina. He turned and froze, his eyes wide in complete horror. Through the blinding glare of the oncoming headlights, the boy thought he saw two people; the driver, with his hands over his face, and the dark outline of a passenger.

"Noooo ... !" Gene screamed.

In that moment, the hand of the mysterious passenger grabbed the wheel before Gene's eyes could even register the action. The wheel was jerked to the side, and within a heartbeat, the car swerved and so narrowly missed the boy, that the wake of the Cortina nearly knocked him off his feet.

There was a sharp, gut-churning screech of tyres, and the Cortina suddenly shuddered to a halt along Church Lane – minus one passenger! The lugubrious stranger had vanished. Gene shakily parked his vehicle and jumped out. The rain had stopped, and he started to walk homewards, a sober man. The three boys who had foolishly hurried in front of the Cortina ran after him.

"Nutter!" shouted the boy who should have died under the wheels.

As delayed shock set in, Gene turned to the boy and, ignoring his taunts, asked: "Did you see a man in that car with me just then?"

"Yeah. So what?" said the boy, discomfited by his odd manner.

He backed away from Gene, calling him a madman as he scurried back to his waiting pals, but his insults seemed to fall on deaf ears, because the man who had almost ended his life, walked silently away up the dark road, staring vacantly ahead.

Gene was so badly affected by the terrifying paranormal experience, that soon afterwards he gave the Cortina away. After breaking down in tears on his return home to his terraced home in Noctorum, Gene told his wife about his unbelievable encounter with Death. She had never known him to lie, or to hold the remotest interest in the occult, so she believed his strange tale.

Nowadays when Gene has a drink, he makes sure a taxi takes him home!

## The Haunted Wardrobe

In my experience of supernatural encounters, I have come to realise that ghosts can attach themselves to just about anything, and the following story illustrates this point.

In the early 1970s, *The Sun* newspaper asked its readers to relate any encounters with the supernatural which they may have had, and were inundated with many strange tales from people from all walks of life, from the length and breadth of the country. I received a clipping of one particular incident that a reader from Birkenhead related to the newspaper, and here's what the reader, a Mrs Barbara Manning of Birkenhead, reported:

> We bought an old wardrobe from a friend of my mother-in-law's who had died. This lady was about eighty with very white hair. After it had been installed I woke up one night around 1am, and, by the wardrobe, a white-haired old lady was standing. She moved towards the wardrobe door and opened it and started to hunt about inside it. She stayed there for a while and took quite a time as though she was searching for something. Then she vanished. One minute she was there, next moment she had gone.

Another incident occurred when I was going down a flight of stairs from the top flat in which we then lived. I looked round and there, gazing over the banisters was the same old lady looking down at me. I started to go back up the stairs, and as I got near the top she suddenly disappeared.

On both occasions I was not at all frightened, perhaps because the figures appeared to me to be quite solid, though a little hazy. No more incidents have happened since then, so I suppose she must have found what she was looking for in the wardrobe.

At the time of the ghostly encounters, Mrs Manning was living in a property (now demolished) near Rock Ferry. I was intrigued by this, because, in August 2000, a woman named Agatha, from Woodhey, which lies less than half a mile from Rock Ferry, called me at Radio Merseyside, minutes after I had been talking about ghosts on the *Billy Butler Show*. Agatha claimed that the house she had lived in was haunted. She had been so utterly frightened that she had vacated the property.

Agatha said that she and her partner Don had moved into the house off Town Lane. Don had decorated the place, and had bought various items of furniture for the house, including a quaint old wardrobe, which he put in their bedroom.

Two days after the couple had moved into the house, at about 1.30am, Agatha and Don were lying in bed, discussing what they needed to buy next. Suddenly, Agatha's face turned very pale, and in a trembling low voice, murmured: "Don! Look!"

Don followed her frozen gaze and recoiled. An old snowy-haired woman was with them in their room. She had her back to Don and Agatha, and seemed to be trying to turn the handle of the antique wardrobe. The handle squeaked, and the woman succeeded in opening the wardrobe door.

Don jumped up out bed. Standing opposite the woman, wearing only his boxer shorts, he shouted: "Hey! What're you doing?"

Agatha let out a scream, as the woman turned and fled behind the wardrobe. Don dashed to the light-switch and clicked on the light. The elderly woman had vanished into thin air. The couple were so shaken by the ghostly intruder, that they decided to sleep in the spare room. On the following night, Agatha and Don returned to their bedroom – with their dog, Bobby – a two-year-old Aberdeen terrier. Don thought it was a bad idea, but Agatha was absolutely terrified, and insisted on allowing Bobby to sleep at the bottom of the bed. She left the bedside lamp on all night.

At 2.15am, the couple were jolted out of their sleep by the sound of Bobby barking, snapping and growling. Agatha and Don grabbed one another, and, fearing the worst, peeped over the blankets to see something that would send them running out of that room.

The old woman was back, and now she was floating in mid-air, half way up the wardrobe, and she was smiling at the hysterical terrier. To this day Agatha has no memory of running out of the room, but Don remembers it vividly:

"I grabbed Agatha, who was screaming hysterically, and I don't know where I got the strength from, but I picked her up out of the bed and ran out of the room with Bobby barking at my bare feet. As I went down the landing outside, I heard the old woman's ghost cackling. Even thinking about it now sends a cold shiver down my spine."

Understandably, the couple refused to stay in the house, and soon moved to Dacre Hill. Had they known about the wardrobe's spooky reputation, maybe they could have thrown *it* out instead and stayed in the house.

The whereabouts of that haunted wardrobe is still unknown. Could it be the old wardrobe in *your* bedroom?

## Strange Apparitions

Not far from Ledsham, there is a winding country lane near the A540 that runs from Puddington to the celebrated Ness Gardens. This road is said to be haunted by a peculiar ghost – the phantom of a motorcyclist who has his head on the wrong way round! The origin of this tale is said to be in a tragic accident that allegedly took place on the road in the 1930s. A man named Hatherton drove a motorcycle and sidecar up and down the lane regularly as he visited his sweetheart – the daughter of a Burton farmer. One bitterly cold night, she let Hatherton borrow her brother's coat, but it was a bit too small, and he couldn't button it up because it was so tight. The girl told her boyfriend to put the coat on back to front so the freezing cold, knife-edged wind wouldn't give him pleurisy.

Hatherton put the coat on back to front, kissed his girlfriend, and rode off through the wintry night. At a sharp bend in the road the bike and its sidecar slid out of control, and hit a tree. A slow-witted but brawny farm labourer came upon the wreckage, and saw Hatherton lying unconscious, face down in a ditch. The bike and the wreckage of the sidecar covered Hatherton's legs. The boy didn't realise that the coat was being worn back to front. He thought the driver's neck was broken, and when he heard Hatherton moaning, the labourer made a desperate attempt to twist the head the right way round. He broke Hatherton's neck.

Not long afterwards, people travelling on that stretch of road after dark reported seeing a motorcycle and sidecar being driven by a man with his head twisted around 180 degrees.

~

A ghost that is arguably stranger than the last two is said to haunt a certain street in Birkenhead, where an old club once stood. The club showcased variety acts, but new houses now stand on the spot so I have to be careful; I don't want to frighten the present inhabitants. In the 1970s, an elderly performer who went under various stage names in the course of his cabaret career, dreamt up a character called Frederick – a six-foot-tall baby in a huge napkin (and pin) and an old-fashioned petal-rimmed baby bonnet. With a rattle in his hand, Frederick was about to make his debut on stage, when the comic portraying him died unexpectedly from thrombosis of the brain. He died alone and in great agony in the dressing room of the club, where he was found in a pool of blood.

The club was closed for three days as a mark of respect, but when it reopened, a well-known comedy duo who had never performed at the club before were amused to see a man dressed as a baby walking around backstage. They asked the management who he was, but were met only with silence and gasps. After the comics had performed their act and been paid, the management told them about the recent tragedy concerning Frederick. The frightened comedy duo never appeared at that club again.

A singer and comedian who was unlucky enough to see the 'big baby' at close quarters as he was setting up his public address system, said he saw blood gush down the face of the apparition, bubbling from its nose.

As recently as May 2002, Glenys, Patsy and Rob – three residents who live near to the spot where the old variety club used to stand – asked me if I had ever heard of the ghost of a man dressed as a baby. I told them about Frederick, and they said that they had seen him looking through the window of a house in the early hours of the morning. At first they thought it was someone playing a prank, but then the figure inexplicably vanished into an alleyway. Patsy mentioned the bizarre-looking ghost to her Special Constable boyfriend, and he admitted that he had also seen the ghost months back, but had told no one because he was sure that no one would believe him!

## The Reunion

The following eerie tale was related to me by Graham, from Leasowe.

In 1978, Graham left school, aged 16, and went to London to work for his uncle in a shoe shop. A few years later he went through a succession of jobs in the capital, but ironically ended up marrying a fellow Wirralian, a student from West Kirby who had been studying at a London college. In 1998, Graham and his wife decided to move back to Wirral, and upon his return home, he saw a notice in the local newspaper informing him that members of the class of '78 were invited to a school reunion to be held at a club in Leasowe.

Graham decided to attend the reunion, and as he drove from his modest home in Hoylake to Leasowe, he wondered if any of his old classmates had become successful. Graham was working for a software company, but he wasn't exactly Bill

Gates. It was a struggle to pay the mortgage, and because of the unpredictability of computer technology, his future financial stability was not a certainty. Perhaps some of the lads he had shared a classroom with so long ago would be millionaires by now. Perhaps some of them would still have all of their hair intact; Graham's hairline had receded quite a few inches since the late 1970s.

At 7.30pm, Graham arrived in the club parking lot. As he secured his vehicle, he met an old friend who was unmistakably the adult version of his old best friend, Brian. The two men squinted at each other by the faint light of a sodium lamppost, then Brian grinned. Graham's friend from so long ago had put on a lot of weight, but the smiling face and mischievous eyes seemed the same. The two men didn't have to say a word, they simply hugged each other. Then they simultaneously pinched each other's bottom, a juvenile ritual from a bygone decade of lost innocence.

"Ouch!" Graham yelled.

It was so good to see his best friend's sense of fun was still intact. Some old friends Graham had already bumped into had lost all their childhood traits. It was as if the hardships of adulthood had lobotomised them and removed their sense of wonder at the magic of life.

Graham and Brian strolled together into the club and found an assembly of vaguely familiar men. Slowly, the old names came flooding back. At the centre of the group was the man who had once been the school bully. His name was Lawrence, but Graham couldn't recall if that had been his first name or his surname. You never inquired, or wanted to know in 1975, when he had you in a painful headlock! Graham had been so terrified of him, that he had once planned to kill him. He had taken the cover off a light switch in the classroom, hoping that Lawrence would automatically carry out his usual trick of flicking the lights on and off to achieve a discotheque effect, whenever he entered the room. True to form, one afternoon he carelessly placed his hands on the light switch and 240 volts shot up his arm, violently flinging him through the classroom doorway into the corridor. That afternoon, a horrified, guilt-stricken Graham prayed for the bully to survive, and fortunately, Lawrence merely got to his feet and smiled, saying, "Wow, did you see that?"

As Graham looked at the 36-year-old version of Lawrence, he saw that time and life had punished him for all those Chinese burns, toilet duckings and extortion rackets. Lawrence had shaved his head, but not because he preferred the look. From the faint tell-tale shadows on his scalp, you could plainly see the permanently receded hairline which the decades had given him. The grown-up bully also had a beer gut, double chin, and worst of all, an appalling sense of taste, evident in the gold sovereign rings he wore on each forefinger and the chunky gold bracelets that decked his thick wrist. The red, white and blue tracksuit, emblazoned with a popular logo, was suited to a much younger man, and therefore made Lawrence look even older and faintly ridiculous.

"Hello possum!" said a voice behind Graham, attempting a terrible imitation of Dame Edna Everage.

Graham and Brian turned simultaneously and saw that it was Rory – the joker of the class. The memories came flooding back in a landslide. In the school science lab, Rory had once fed a hose from a Bunsen burner into a sink full of Fairy Liquid and created a foaming mass of inflammable hydrogen bubbles which he ignited with a taper, thus illustrating how a mushroom cloud forms when hydrogen explodes. Hair and eyebrows were singed, and the ceiling of the science lab remained blackened for years. Just one of a succession of Rory's pranks.

Brian and Graham shook hands with Rory, half-suspecting his palm to contain a wound-up buzzer. The former classroom clown said he was delighted that he could make the reunion. He had only arrived in Wirral two weeks ago after flying from Sydney, where he now lived. "That explains the Dame Edna impressions!" Graham thought to himself. He also noticed that Rory was looking incredibly good – he had barely aged at all.

The reunion went very well. Precious memories and jokes were exchanged until a quarter to nine, when someone suggested they should go to an old pub situated near their former school. Before the men set off, a few of them remarked that one notable member of the class of '78 had not arrived. His name was Tony. He was remembered because he had such amazing artistic skills, and could draw all of the super-heroes from the *Marvel* and *DC* comics – including the voluptuous super-heroines. He'd surely be a graphic designer or illustrator by now.

Minutes after the reunited classmates arrived at the pub, Tony walked in, and was greeted by a resounding cheer that startled the regulars. He hadn't changed very much. His coal-black hair contained a few glinting grey hairs, and he now sported a goatee beard, but he was unmistakably Tony. He was hugged and patted and ushered to the front until he stood between Graham and Brian. A long conversation about the halcyon days of the school playground ensued; then Tony made a strange remark.

"It's a pity about Rory, isn't it?" he said, gazing pensively at the foam shapes on the surface of his lager.

"What do you mean?" asked Graham.

He thought for a moment that Tony was going to tell him that Rory had a terminal illness.

"Oh, don't you know?" Tony said, casting a melancholy glance at him.

"Know what?" replied Graham, leaning forward.

"He died in a car crash in Australia."

Graham and Brian gazed at one another and shook their heads.

"But he's here," said Brian, searching in vain for Rory's face among the crowd.

"No way," said Tony. "He died in a car crash in 1988. Someone even showed me a newspaper clipping of the article."

"Bet you a hundred quid you're wrong," said Graham, offering his hand to Tony with a smug grin.

"You're on!"

Tony accepted the wager with an equally eager handshake.

Graham went off in search of Rory. He checked the parlour. He wasn't there. He checked the bar. He was nowhere to be seen. The men's toilets were also checked, but Rory couldn't be found there either. Knowing how much of a joker he was, Graham sneaked into the ladies' loo and quickly discovered that his missing friend wasn't there either. Brian checked the carpark, and then looked up and down the street. Rory was definitely nowhere to be found.

Graham gathered together the people who had talked with Rory and who had seen him at the club. Lawrence confirmed that he had been at the club, and so did about fourteen other people. Yet Tony remained adamant that Rory had died ten years ago.

"Okay, alright, I'm going to get the article that states in black and white that he died in a car crash in Sydney in 1988. Wait there," said Tony, seriously.

The crowd laughed as they watched Tony leave the pub to get a cab. Sure enough, he returned half an hour later with a confident expression on his face. From the top pocket of his jacket he produced a yellowed newspaper cutting. He placed it on the bar and traced his finger along the headlines and the text as spectacles were promptly put on. The article did indeed state that Rory, from Leasowe, had been killed in a head-on collision with a truck on a stretch of highway near Sydney in 1988.

"Think yourself lucky I don't hold you to that bet," Tony said to Graham, who was reading and re-reading the clipping with a puzzled look.

Graham and Brian later conducted their own research. Brian visited Rory's sister in Wallasey, and she confirmed that her brother had died in an automobile crash in August 1988. Graham visited the micro-filmed newspaper archives of a library to obtain photocopies of two other articles detailing the crash in which Rory had perished. He and Brian, and several other people who had attended the reunion that night, came to the unsettling conclusion that Rory had somehow returned from beyond the grave to be reunited with his old school friends.


## Warning from a Dead Rock Star

In September 1988, Janice and David, a married couple in their twenties from Leasowe, went to visit relatives in the London district of Barnes. On the Friday night of 16 September 1988, the couple were forced to leave their relations at the unearthly hour of 3.45 in the morning. After receiving an urgent and emotional phone call from their daughter, Hazel, they had to head back to Wirral. Janice's mother was seriously ill after suffering a stroke.

At four in the morning, they were travelling up Queen's Ride, a road that runs through Barnes Common. A distraught Janice was telling David that he should have taken another route towards Hammersmith, but he had insisted on a route that would take them across Putney Bridge. As they were discussing, rather heatedly, the best route home, a car came speeding past them. It tore down Queen's Ride at a phenomenal speed towards the hump-backed bridge. As Janice was screaming at the reckless driver, David noticed that the car was a dark-coloured Mini, and he even managed to glance at the first half of the registration plate, which read 'FOX'.

"He's not going to make it," David whispered under his breath.

Then he watched in horror as the Mini hurtled forward at great speed towards the hump-backed bridge.

When the mini hit the top of the bridge it went sailing into the air. There was an unnerving sense of quiet for a second or two, before the couple both flinched; there was a huge blast of noise as the speeding car violently crashed into something – possibly a tree. The vehicle's headlights swept and swirled awkwardly over the surrounding trees as the Mini spun around and impacted into the tree.

David slowed right down and crawled slowly over the hump-backed bridge, not sure what to expect on the other side. However, there was no sign of the crashed Mini. David was positive that the driver could not possibly have survived that crash and driven on into the night. Janice wound down the window and gazed out into the silent darkness. She too could see no evidence of a car crash whatsoever. With more pressing matters to contend with, the couple had to simply drive on, reaching Wirral later that day. Fortunately, Janice's mother made a rapid recovery from the stroke over the following months, with the love and support of her family.

~

In the November of that same year, David was in his local library, flipping through the pages of a book about pop stars, when he came upon a piece of information that chilled him to the bone. One of the stars mentioned in the book was the late glam-rock star, Marc Bolan, lead singer of T Rex. The book mentioned the details surrounding the singer's death. It plainly stated that in 1977, in the early hours of Friday 16 September, Marc Bolan had died in a purple Mini 1275 GT, licence plate FOX 66IL – on Queen's Ride, Barnes Common.

David swore with disbelief as readers and two librarians looked up at him. According to the book, Bolan's partner, Gloria Jones, had been at the wheel of the Mini, and had lost control at a hump-backed bridge. The vehicle had smashed through a fence and crashed into a sycamore tree. The passenger side of the Mini took the main impact, and Marc was thrown into the back of the car. His death was instantaneous, but Gloria miraculously survived. The official cause of Bolan's death was shock and haemorrhage due to multiple injuries consistent with a road traffic accident.

David could not believe what he was reading. He took the book out and couldn't wait to show it to Janice, for his own sanity's sake, if nothing else. She was just as amazed as he was when she saw the article. David was so fascinated by the whole affair that he carried out further research into the Bolan death smash and discovered that it had taken place just after four in the morning – the exact time that he and Janice had encountered the mysterious vanishing Mini.

The couple returned to Barnes Common the following summer and visited the sycamore tree where Bolan had met his death. The tree was covered with floral tributes from fans of the late singer, and Janice also left six red roses at the tree. David and Janice remain completely unable to explain what happened on that chilling September night when they apparently witnessed a ghostly re-enactment of the crash, but Janice thinks it may have been a warning from Bolan himself. David was speeding down Queen's Ride that night, in a rush to get home, and could have easily lost control at the hump-backed bridge, because he was not familiar with that stretch of road.

## The Frankby Phantom and the Ghost of Greasby

When it's foggy in Frankby, stay indoors if you fear the supernatural, for when nature's shroud covers the landscape, even during the hours of daylight, strange uncanny beings go on the prowl …

In December 2000, a freezing fog crept inland from the Irish Sea and invaded Wirral from the north-west. Visibility was reduced to less than a hundred metres in places such as Hoylake, Moreton, Greasby and Frankby. On the Friday night of 29 December 2000, at 9.20pm, Josh Osborn, an amateur astronomer, and his friend, Paul, were sitting on deckchairs in a bleak field near Yew Tree Farm in Frankby. The two men – both in their twenties – were clad in fur-lined fleece jackets and wore thermal socks beneath their wellington boots. In their gloved hands they held binoculars, through which they eagerly peered at the starry winter sky. Earlier that month there had been a UFO sighting over Frankby, and as Josh and Paul had an interest in the fascinating subject of ufology, they had decided to hold a vigil in the field, in the hope of spotting the mysterious visitor to Frankby's skies.

A point of light appeared in the heavens. It seemed stationary at first, then moved rapidly to the left at an estimated speed of about a hundred miles per hour. It was coming in from over the Irish Sea, heading towards Liverpool. The binoculars were trained on the unidentified object, then the two men sighed with disappointment as they realised what the UFO really was. The green and red port and starboard lights were now visible, as well as the white flashing tail-rudder light that is required by international aviation law. Then came the faint drone of the Cessna light aircraft engine. The object had been nothing more exciting than an aeroplane.

The two UFO spotters heard a whirring sound nearby. They looked back to earth and saw the silhouette of a man, pedalling furiously on a bicycle down Frankby Road. The dynamo of his speeding racer bike kindled a steady bright red glow in the tail-light.

Then came the 'thing', hard on the cyclist's tail.

Josh and Paul looked on in disbelief. A white, vaporous form, that resembled the top half of a man with outstretched arms and swathed in a white blanket, was hovering about four feet off the ground in close pursuit of the frantic cyclist. The man's legs were a blur as he pedalled his bike round the curve of the road. The eerie pursuer fluttered after him. At this point, the fog rolled inland from the sea, and the stalked cyclist, and the unearthly apparition chasing him, both faded into the shadowy mists, until the red point of the bike's rear light dimmed into total obscurity.

"What the heck was that?" said Paul at last, gazing down the road into the fog with his binoculars.

"The Frankby Phantom," said Josh, thumbing the focus wheel of the binoculars as he squinted through its lenses. It was no use; the fog was too dense to allow a glimpse of the fleeing cyclist.

Josh had heard about the Frankby Phantom many years before when he was 12 years old. His grandfather had told him that it flew down Montgomery Hill on some moonlit nights to attack late-night travellers. Some said it was the restless ghost of a man who had been laid to rest in nearby Frankby Cemetery, but no one was sure what the phantom was. When motor cars began to travel on the roads round Frankby in the 1930s, the phantom often chased them, and is said to have caused several fatal crashes in the area.

~

In 1950, a man named Mr Clare left a pub in the area just after midnight and was walking homewards up Hill Bark Road, when he saw an amorphous pale object which came hurtling towards him down the road with a fluttering sound. Mr Clare turned on his heels and ran back to the pub as fast as his legs would carry him. The terrified Frankby man glanced over his shoulder as he fled back to the pub, and saw the ectoplasmic entity gaining on him. He tripped and fell flat on his face, and the ghost flew over him, banked in the air, turned gracefully with a waltzing movement, then came speeding back towards him. Mr Clare jumped to his feet and ran screaming towards the pub. He reached the inn and hammered on the door, and the landlord, recognising the voice of his regular customer, unbolted and yanked open the oaken door. Mr Clare barged into the pub, with the Frankby Phantom still following close behind. The landlord slammed the door and started to bolt it when something crashed into it. The impact almost threw the door off its cast iron hinges. The four remaining drinkers at the pub shuddered as the supernatural being tapped heavily on each of the windows. One brave drinker was about to pull aside the heavy curtains to catch a glimpse of the hostile phantasm, but the landlord seized his hand and prevented him from taking a look. No one dared leave that pub until the pale milky light of dawn arrived. There have been many more encounters with the Frankby Phantom, but to date, no ghost researcher has discovered why the strange being is haunting Frankby.

As for Josh and Paul, they were so unnerved by the vision that they quickly folded up their deckchairs, gathered their cameras and binoculars, and hurried to Josh's car before the Frankby Phantom returned from haunting the unfortunate cyclist. They quickly drove home to Saughall Massie, and were thankful to reach their destination unscathed.

~

It was on a similar night in neighbouring Greasby, in the October of 1992, when an insidious jade fog blanketed the streets and lanes. Mrs Kayse, and her 12-year-old daughter Christina, were hurrying home after visiting a relative on the Green Acres Estate. The time was shortly after midnight, and the mother and daughter only had to travel up Milk Lane to their home off Greasby's Arrowe Road, about a quarter of a mile away. Not a single person, or car, passed by during this time. As Christina and her mother walked up the silent, fog-enshrouded road, they became aware of a strange whimpering somewhere in the distance. It sounded like a baby crying. The noise alarmed them, for who would take a baby out on the streets on a freezing, cold, foggy night?

Then they saw the faint outline of a person approaching. It was a tall woman wearing a headscarf. She pushed a large, outdated perambulator with a huge hood. Its wheels squeaked as it rumbled along. The woman's clothes were as out of vogue as the old pram. She wore a long salt and pepper-coloured coat that almost reached down to meet her fur-lined ankle boots. She looked as if she was in her seventies, yet moved agilely along the pavement with the pram. Her face was tawny coloured and her eyes were wide and stared ahead of her with an eerie menace. When she looked down and saw Christina holding on to her mother's hand, the woman smiled and stopped in her tracks.

Christina stared in horror at the weird-looking old woman and clutched at her mother's arm with both hands.

"Come here!" the woman suddenly screamed, and she let go of the pram's handle and lunged at Christina.

Christina yelped. Her mother was equally afraid of the grotesque and frightening old woman, and started to run away, pulling her daughter along with her. Mrs Kayse dared to steal a glance back at the maniacal woman and saw her grabbing what seemed to be a knife from the pram. The sight gave Mrs Kayse a feeling of intense fear in the pit of her stomach, and she picked up Christina, who was now crying, and fled up Milk Lane. Mrs Kayse looked back once more, and, to her horror, she saw the old woman creeping up the lane, keeping close to the wall, like a rat, as she stalked them, with a knife in her hand.

Further along the lane was a church, and Mrs Kayse had a feeling that the evil old woman would not be able to pursue her past the hallowed ground. Her intuition proved to be true. The knife-wielding weirdo turned and vanished back into the mists of the night before she reached the church.

Mrs Kayse later discovered that several other people had seen the pram-pushing woman in other parts of Greasby, and most encounters were said to have taken place during thick fog. Curiously, in a majority of the confrontations with the old hag, there is never another pedestrian or a vehicle on the road, almost as if time has come to a standstill. Some of the older folk in Greasby think that she is the ghost of an old woman who was said to have snatched several babies from their prams back in Victorian times. If you live in Frankby or Greasby, keep your children safe on foggy nights.

## The Thumb

The people of Wirral and the rest of the north west of England never cease to amaze me with their extensive knowledge of local incidents. When the best search engines of the world-wide web fail me, I turn to the human internet of people, by posing a query on air at the radio station, or within my *Local Mysteries* column of the *Merseymart and Star*. The answer I am seeking is usually soon forwarded to me by a listener or a reader. An example, is the following suspense-filled tale, which I unearthed whilst researching the bizarre case of a phantom severed bloody thumb that is often seen to materialise on the counter of a certain Wirral public house. I mentioned the surreal apparition on the *Billy Butler Show* and received a deluge of telephone calls and emails explaining the reasons behind the appearance of the severed digit.

The tale I have pieced together concerns a daredevil who we will call Warren. He was once an incurable adrenaline junkie and one of those rare individuals for whom fear is not an option. Whilst parachuting over Belgium in the 1960s, both his main and reserve chutes failed, so with amazing reflexes, he aimed himself at a fellow parachutist and slammed into him, almost knocking him unconscious. He clung on to his winded colleague and opened his chute for him, and the two made it to earth safely. In the mid-1970s, Warren signed a three-year contract to serve as a mercenary in Rhodesia, earning just £40 per week. In 1978, after serving his term, he returned home to his native Heswall, where he became the licensee of a pub.

Few of his regulars were aware of his adventurous past, but in that summer of 1978, an event was to take place that would show the locals just how fearless and steely-nerved Warren really was. It all started on Poll Hill, the highest point in Wirral, one burning July day, when a landslide of motorcycles rumbled down the hill. A deep-throated roar came from the engines of the Harley-Davidsons, a BSA

29

Lightning Rocket, a Triumph Thunderbird and a Bonneville, followed by a phalanx of other bikes; their chrome dazzling in the noonday sun. At first the locals thought the bikers were some chapter of the Hell's Angels, but the riders coming down Poll Hill were just a motley collection of troublemakers from West Kirby, New Brighton and Moreton, on a run to Flintshire. They had been in the saddle for almost two hours as they filed down the road, gliding over the undulating mirage on the tarmaca surface in the shimmering heat – towards Warren's pub.

The six-foot-three, 19-stone leader of the gang wore the typical biker's uniform of a German helmet, sepia shades, leather jacket sporting a swastika of metal studs, greasy Levis and oversized Doc Marten boots. He was called Big Donny, also known as Donny the Menace, as well as Dirty Don! He cruised to a halt in the pub carpark, missing parked vehicles by inches. Twelve other bikes revved low and came to rest in the carpark as well. Donny kicked the stand of his bike down and walked like a gunslinger towards the pub, flanked on each side by his henchman. A student who was innocently sipping a coke outside the pub with his girlfriend, was grabbed by his long locks and thrown over the carpark wall for no reason at all. The lad's girlfriend yelled at Donny, but he just barged past her into the pub, making a rude gesture as he did so.

Fortunately, there were only two drinkers in the pub that afternoon: an old man named Ralph, and a young blonde-haired woman named Jayne, who was dating Warren. Warren stood behind the bar by the till, eyeing the ruffians closely.

Donny removed his helmet to reveal a head of long greasy hair. He seemed to be gazing at Jayne, but it was hard to know exactly what he was looking at, because he was wearing sunglasses. As the rest of the gang thumped the counter and noisily demanded drinks, Donny suddenly reached out towards Jayne.

His tattooed arm was seized in the blink of an eye by Warren.

"Oh! no, you don't! You can look – but you'd better not touch," he warned.

Donny pulled his arm away, and his twelve disciples reached into their leathers for coshes, Stanley knives and chains.

"Do you want this place smashed up, mate?" Donny asked, rubbing his arm where the ex-mercenary's iron grip had dug into his flesh.

"No, I don't," Warren replied, keeping cool and apparently unruffled.

Donny lunged towards Jayne again, and as the girl backed away, Warren intervened once again.

"No you don't, mate!" he shouted.

"Have you got a death wish?" Donny asked, trying to keep up his bravado, but feeling decidedly uneasy in the company of this cooly confrontational barman.

Warren smiled and nodded enthusiastically, then bent down and produced a large meat cleaver which made every onlooker recoil. The licensee kept the weapon under the counter for such occasions.

Donny the Menace recoiled when he saw the cold steel of the chopper and instinctively took a step backwards.

"You're outnumbered, pal," he said.

"I take it you're the leader?" Warren inquired calmly.

After a thoughtful pause, Donny nodded slowly, "Yes, I am."

"Well, if you're a man, you'll accept a challenge, from me to you, man to man," said Warren, with a deadpan expression.

"What're you talking about?"

Donny laughed uneasily and looked to his followers to back him up, but all their eyes were on the glinting chopper blade.

"How about a wager?" said Warren, his voice devoid of emotion. "And if you win, you take this pub, lock, stock and barrel, and you take Jayne here as well."

Jayne swore, about to plead with him, "Warren …"

"Quiet," the licensee ordered, without taking his gaze from Donny's face.

"You're crazy, man," said Donny, and he urged his gang to attack with a nod of the head, but Warren intervened.

"If just one of you lifts a finger, I will jump over this bar and put this cleaver through your forehead," he told Donny, in a matter-of-fact way.

"You'll be dead," said Donny, globules of sweat oozing from his face.

"I'd love to die, it'd be a welcome change. But I swear to God I'll split your greasy head open first – right down the greasy centre-part. Just try me. Go on – try me."

There was a long pause. Jayne trembled as she watched the tense stand-off.

"You going to accept the wager, or are you a coward?"

Donny let rip a string of expletives and swore that he was not a coward.

"Okay then, here's the deal," said Warren, patting the cold steel of the meat cleaver against his hot perspiring face. "I put a playing card on the dart board; the three of clubs. I give you three darts. If you get them into each of the three pips, you can have this pub, you can have my girl, and you can have my new Jeep into the bargain."

"You're as nutty as a fruit cake," said Donny.

The gang leader was becoming increasingly concerned about the way his lackeys were holding back, almost as if they wanted him to take up the sensational challenge.

"If you fail to get three darts into three pips, I cut off your thumb with this." Warren said, gently tapping the varnished bar counter with the cleaver blade.

Donny swore and turned to his gang of bikers.

"It's impossible to do that with the darts. It's like a fairground trick."

"So you're scared then. You're supposed to be the leader of the gang and you're terrified of losing your thumb. What a yellow-bellied coward," jeered Warren.

"Donny isn't yellow," said Gut, an obese gang member, through gritted teeth. "Do it, Donny. Then you'll have this loser's pub *and* his girl!"

"… and his Jeep," mumbled a bearded biker with a face criss-crossed with scars from when he had drunkenly driven his motorcycle through a shop window. They called him Plate Glass.

"Gut! Plate! Be quiet!" spat Donny, feeling confused and decidedly scared. It was a crazy situation. The odds were stacked against him.

"You look scared, Donny," said Jayne, edging backwards by inches. She was terrified that if Donny did manage to land a dart in each pip of the playing card, she'd probably be attacked by the intimidating gang.

Donny's eyebrows dipped to his nose with anger as he pointed at the blonde girl.

"Nobody, especially a woman, calls me a coward. Nobody!"

"Well, come on then! Take up the challenge you lily-livered failure!"

Warren's boldness made Donny and his people jump.

An assortment of expletives and mumblings came from the gang, and Gut and Plate Glass encouraged Donny to accept the cleaver-wielding licensee's dare.

"Okay!"

Donny had convinced himself that if he lost the wager, he could escape without losing his thumb. His leather-clad mates wouldn't give Warren a chance to use the chopper.

Jayne dashed behind the bar. Warren kept his eye on the bikers as he reached for the pack of playing cards on the shelf. He handed the deck to Jayne and told her to locate the three of clubs. Jayne shakily shuffled through the pack and located the card. She handed it to Warren, and he passed it to Plate Glass, and told him to slide it into the wireframe of the dartboard.

The three of clubs was placed vertically on the dartboard, and Jayne handed the three darts to Donny, who seemed to fumble with them, and made weak remarks about the condition of the flights and the lightness of the barrels.

"Get on with it, Donny. Stop making excuses. Those flights are brand new," said Warren, relentlessly tapping the counter with the chopper.

Donny took off his shades to reveal a pair of shifty blue eyes. He stood with the toe of his Doc Martens on the seven foot marker line on the darts mat and turned to Warren.

"I'm a bit rusty, so how about a bit of practice?"

After a long pause, Warren replied: "Okay. You can have three throws, then it's the real thing."

Jayne glared at Warren as her heart thumped. The first dart hit the centre pip of the card. A cheer went up from the gang.

"Shut up!" roared Donny, and he threw the second dart.

The second dart was deflected off the barrel of the first one, and it went straight into the top pip.

Plate Glass punched the air and cried, "Yahoo!"

Gut clamped his large tattooed hand across Plate's bearded face. Jayne began to feel dizzy with fear, and Warren's face twitched in nervous anticipation.

"This isn't a practice, man," threatened Donny, with sweat dripping from his brow. "This is the real thing."

"No, Donny, this is the practice, and if you're a man of honour, you'll keep to your word," said Warren.

Donny hurled the dart. It hit the card – in the white. It landed a centimetre from the bottom pip. The gang let out a sigh in unison. Gut collected the darts and handed them back to Donny.

"Now, *this* is the real thing, Donny," Warren said, as if Donny needed a reminder.

Donny took up position again on the mat, and held the dart in the air, moving his forearm gently back and forth. One of the bikers coughed involuntarily, so Danny spat at him and aggressively waved him out of the way. He shook his head, then meditated for a while. He remembered the philosophy of the Zen Buddhists, who say that a man should act without thought, as thought often hinders action. Donny inhaled deeply and threw the dart, and it landed in one of the leaves of the top pip.

"Yes!" someone whispered, and another voice urged him to be quiet.

Donny took up position at the mat again, and nibbled at his knuckle as he squeezed his eyes shut. He looked up at the dartboard, then threw the dart very carefully. The dart seemed to float across the seven feet of space. It pierced the bottom pip of the playing card, right in its centre.

A cheer welled up from the gang, but Warren disputed the hit. However, when the licensee walked to the end of the bar, he could see from the new vantage point that the dart's tip had landed in the pip by a fraction of an inch.

Then, amidst all the tension, the door opened, and a small child walked into the public house. It was a girl of 12 with long black hair and a white tee shirt with a smiley face on it; she was Jayne's niece, Fleur. She looked at Warren, clutching the meat cleaver, and at her Aunt Jayne, cowering behind him, and then she saw the gang of oddly-dressed strangers. She guessed something was amiss, and she turned and tried to run out of the pub, but one of the bikers seized the child by her hair and dragged her back indoors. He threw her down and stood in the doorway, barring any intended exit.

"Leave her alone!" Jayne screamed.

Fleur got up and ran to her aunt, sobbing.

"Shut that kid up!" said Donny, holding the all-important, last dart.

Jayne hugged Fleur and stroked her hair, whispering reassurances. As the child quietened down, Donny took up his stance on the mat. All eyes were on the card. All he had to do was bounce that dart in between the darts in the board, and it would be guided straight into the pip.

Tears rolled from Jayne's eyes, and although Warren turned and winked at her, she couldn't stop trembling.

The dart was thrown as Warren turned back to look at Donny.

It went into the pip. However, it didn't go into the middle one. The dart landed in the top pip, which had already been hit.

"I did it," Donny murmured with obvious relief.

"No! I said each dart had to go into each pip, and you didn't do it," Warren insisted, adopting a defensive stance in front of Jayne and Fleur.

"You didn't say that!" Donny bellowed. "Now it's time for the pay out."

"Okay, Donny. Then I'm going to have to kill you. If you don't believe me, just give the order to these idiots and I swear this cleaver will end up between your eyes."

Warren's eyes glared with pure hatred and animosity. Donny had been in more fights than he cared to remember, and he had acquired a nose for detecting fear in his victims and adversaries. But he could detect no such emotion in Warren.

"Just say the word, Donny," said Gut, and as he did so Warren made his move with lightning agility – reflexes honed in Rhodesia, where you rarely had a second chance.

In a flash, Warren was over the bar and upon the leader of the pack and he pinned him against the wall, his hand locked around the biker's throat. His other hand was poised to strike with the meat cleaver. Twelve inches of steel blade hovered menacingly in the air, ready to strike at any moment.

No one made a move.

"Jayne," said Warren, keeping his voice low.

"Yes?"

"Go outside with Fleur through the side door. Now!"

Jayne edged her way slowly to the door, pulling Fleur by the arm as she went.

As soon as the two girls had left, Warren related several horror stories about the things he had seen in Africa. Things that still gave him sleepless nights. The psychological warfare had the desired effect, and ten members of the gang quickly made their apologies to Donny and left the pub.

Donny could take the humiliation no more, and he kneed Warren in the groin. Gut and Plate Glass moved in. Gut swung a chain and hit Warren across the face, while Plate produced a 1936 SS dagger and plunged it into Warren's upper arm.

The publican fell to his knees with blood squirting from the wound, and he brought the chopper down on Plate's foot. The biker screamed and moved his slit boot away. He often wore steel toe-capped boots, but not today. The blood oozed in a steady stream out of the neat slit. Donny kicked Warren in the face and the force of the kick sent him reeling backwards, knocking his head against the brass foot-rail of the bar. Gut reached down and triumphantly grabbed the meat cleaver. He turned to brag to Plate, but saw that his friend was hopping about with blood dripping from his boots. His big toe had been virtually severed.

Donny's boot was poised, about to stamp on Warren's face when the licensee grabbed it and twisted hard. Donny crashed down with a thud on to his side. The chopper flew down past Warren's face, so close that he felt a draught as it missed his nose by millimetres. The cleaver's blade embedded itself in the floorboard, and Warren delivered a right uppercut into Plate's groin area.

Warren got to his feet and tried to climb over the bar to grab a bottle, but Donny delivered a kidney punch into his back. Warren turned, grabbed Donny by his ears, and head-butted him. He then swung the dazed gang leader against the bar counter, where he held him by the throat, but a hard vicious blow suddenly hit the back of Warren's head. Plate had tried to bring the cleaver down on Warren's head, but the licensee had stumbled backwards whilst wrestling with Donny, so his head had hit Plate's clenched, chopper-wielding fist instead. In the tussle the cleaver was deflected – landing on the bar, where it sliced through Donny's hand. The blade chopped off his thumb at the carpal joint to the hand, and it happened so swiftly, that Donny only felt a slight sharp pain. He wasn't aware of his missing thumb until he tried to make a fist to throw at Warren.

Before Donny and Plate Glass could move in for the kill, the two doors of the pub flew open simultaneously and police officers dashed in to overpower the thugs. Jayne had telephoned them after escaping from the pub.

Warren and his attackers were taken to hospital to have their wounds treated. Donny's thumb could not be found in the bar, and so it could not be reattached. The loss of his thumb left Donny unable to operate the clutch lever on the handlebar of his beloved Harley, and that, along with the humiliation of the bloody debacle at the pub, is thought to have driven the leader of the motorcycle gang to commit suicide by taking an overdose of sleeping pills three months later.

Shortly after the death, Jayne was at Warren's pub one night, just before twelve o'clock, when she let out a piercing scream. She and several drinkers saw a thumb, twitching on the bar counter. It had emerged from under a Jack Daniels bar towel. When Warren came running downstairs to see what the screams were about, the thumb had vanished, but had left a sticky trail of blood on the counter. Hours later, at around four in the morning, Warren and Jayne were awakened by the sound of the last orders bell. Over the following weeks, the sound of someone laughing was also heard in the bar, long after Warren and his girlfriend had retired for the night. In the end, the ghostly goings-on at the pub were too much for Jayne's nerves, and she gave her boyfriend an ultimatum: leave the premises or lose her. Warren was not prepared to let the ghost win and refused. However, a month later, he was involved in a serious car crash and his injuries forced him to give up the pub.

If recent reports are anything to go by, the Wirral pub is still haunted by the restless ghost of Donny and his severed thumb.


## Race with Death

In July 2001, Jack, a 29-year-old New Brighton man, was waiting at the traffic lights in his old Skoda car. In the lane alongside him was a burnished silver Lexus IS200 – the car of Jack's dreams. Jack wound down the driver's window of the Skoda to allow some air into the sweltering interior. The young shaven-headed youth in the Lexus smiled condescendingly over at the Skoda.

"He can't be more than twenty-five years old," thought Jack, pretending not to notice the other driver. He was jealous of the hi-tech vehicle which no doubt had climate control air-conditioning.

Two young women, both blonde, and dressed in the skimpiest, most revealing outfits, crossed the road slowly and smiled at the driver of the Lexus. Jack was consumed with envy, even though he knew he was being petty.

The lights changed, and before the Skoda had even moved out of neutral, the Lexus was already speeding off down Manor Road.

When Jack got home he started to complain to his girlfriend Heather about their lack of money – they could barely make ends meet, never mind buy luxury cars. She was very surprised, as he had never been one to complain about life that much, and Jack told her about the Lexus driver and the way he had sneered. Heather leaned over him as he grumbled in the armchair, and slowly put her arms around him. She began to kiss his neck and ears in a sensual way.

"I've got you, and that's more important than money," she whispered in his ear.

But Jack cursed and grumpily unwrapped her arms before getting to his feet. He walked to the window and gazed out at the woman who lived in the opposite house. She was parking up her brand new Rover saloon.

"I feel like a total failure, Heather," Jack said, shaking his head downheartedly.

Heather promised that when she finished university she would get a job and she also promised that she'd buy him a car. Jack found little consolation in her promises, and tried to explain that he didn't want her to buy him anything. He wanted something better than this job as a bartender. He was tired of listening to the same old stories from the barflies, collecting glasses, listening to the same music on the pub jukebox, and being a passive smoker on top of all that.

By six o'clock that evening, Jack had cooled down somewhat and had reverted to being the person whom Heather knew and loved. He kissed her and admitted that she was right; money wasn't everything. He cooked a meal for them both then cuddled Heather on the sofa as she watched her favourite soap opera.

As they watched television, Jack suddenly asked: "Do you fancy going to Wales tomorrow? It's my day off."

"Yeah, okay, babe," said Heather, and she kissed him.

That night, after Jack had returned from work, the couple made love, and Heather fell asleep in her boyfriend's arms. Everything seemed perfect when he knew he had the love of this woman. He felt totally content as he drifted into sleep.

Jack had only been asleep for a matter of minutes when he experienced one of the strangest, most terrifying nightmares of his life. The horrifying dream began on a country lane. The rays of sunlight flickered through the trees as Jack sped along in a car. It wasn't his Skoda, but a Lexus – the very one he had seen the youth driving along Manor Road. Sitting next to him was Heather, looking very proud. The road seemed to stretch into infinity, so Jack put his foot down on the accelerator and the car zoomed away and the trees at the side of the road became a green blur. According to the speedometer, the Lexus was travelling at 130 miles per hour, and Jack felt the adrenaline rush as the car rocketed down the lane – then he noticed the face. At the end of the road there was what appeared to be an arched tunnel – but it was actually a huge mouth, and above it were the nose and eye sockets of some gigantic grey skull. The mouth was opening steadily wider, and the car was travelling too fast to stop. The face became clearer and looked positively demonic at closer quarters. Luminous green eyes glowed in the darkness of the cavernous eye sockets, and it was now clear that the interior of the arched tunnel was red and fleshy. Jack pumped the brake but all he heard was the screech of the car's tyres and Heather's screams. The Lexus flew into the gigantic gaping mouth of the skull – Jack yelled out and woke up in a sweat.

"What's wrong?" Heather asked, confused after being startled out of a peaceful sleep.

Jack sat bolt upright in bed and after realising that he had only suffered a nightmare, he related the strange dream to Heather. She cuddled him as he attempted to fall asleep once more. This time he and Heather slept soundly.

On the following morning, after breakfast, the couple set out for a picnic in Wales. As it was a Sunday, the roads weren't too busy, and the Skoda was soon travelling along the rural lanes around Llangollen, where Jack intended to show Heather the ruins of a 13th century castle atop a 1000 foot hill. Jack was driving down the narrow country lane, seven miles from the castle, when he saw a familiar car come alongside him. He was astonished to see that it was the same Lexus he had seen tearing away from the traffic lights on Manor Road. The young man behind the wheel smirked as he slowly overtook Jack's Skoda. Then Jack saw something that chilled him to the bone. There was someone – or something – in the passenger seat. It was a hooded figure wearing a type of monk's cowl. Beneath the cowl was a grey skull – a much smaller version of the skull that had appeared in last night's terrifying dream!

The grotesque and unearthly passenger turned to face Jack and then made a curious and unnerving gesture. It raised and lowered its right arms in such a way as to suggest that Jack should slow down. Jack braked hard and the Skoda screeched to a halt. Heather's hands seized the fascia of the car in horror.

"What did you do that for?" she cried.

Jack told her what he had just seen in the car that was overtaking them, but Heather was dismissive, instead growing concerned and fearful that perhaps her boyfriend was having a nervous breakdown.

However, the Skoda continued on its way, and a short time later, as Jack turned into a sharp bend in the road, he and Heather came upon the wreckage of the Lexus. The car had evidently approached the bend too fast and had hit a wall. Jack left his car to see if he could get the driver out, but he was already dead from his injuries and his body was trapped in the mangled car wreckage. Jack could plainly see that there was no one else in the car, and he realised that the skeletal figure he had seen in the passenger seat, urging him to slow down, had been some personification of Death, perhaps the mythical Grim Reaper himself.

The experience shook Jack up very badly, and he never envied people in flashy fast cars again.

# Ghostly Lock-in

Somewhere in Wirral there stands a pub that has been boarded up for a few years now. There are no takers because the place has gained a supernatural reputation.

In the 1990s, Margaret, a widow, became the licensee of this pub. Unlike many other licensees in the north west, and the rest of England, Margaret refused to entertain stay-behinds, which, as most readers will know, is an almost traditional social event wherein drinkers who are in no hurry to go to their homes, and the greedier customers are given a bonus period of an hour or more after last orders at eleven o'clock. Well, Margaret closed her pub at eleven o'clock sharp, and she forced her customers to drink up and vacate the place.

However, one Halloween night Margaret rang the dreaded last orders bell, and, by eleven o'clock, she and a barmaid were ushering the last die-hard drinkers off the premises. They then performed all the usual clearing up duties: they emptied all the ashtrays, wiped down the table tops in the parlour, cleaned the counters, emptied the till and put the stools up on the seats. At twenty past midnight, the barmaid went home, and soon afterwards, Margaret went to bed to get some well-deserved rest.

At two in the morning the telephone beside her bed started to ring, startling Margaret from her sleep. The phone was an extension of the one downstairs in the bar, so when anyone rang the pub, the two phones rang at the same time. Margaret lifted the receiver to hear a man's voice.

"You're a hypocrite aren't you?"

Margaret didn't understand.

"Pardon?" she asked.

"You threw me out and said you don't have stay-behinds, but you let your cronies have them."

"I don't have stay-behinds," protested Margaret sleepily, as she glanced at her bedside alarm clock.

The man swore and hung up.

Margaret put the phone down. She thought about the strange call for a while, then decided it had been made by some intoxicated customer who had not taken lightly to being forced to leave the premises earlier. She yawned, and was about to switch off the bedside lamp – when she heard voices. Voices which were coming from downstairs. Initially she thought that the voices were coming from the street outside, but she still went downstairs to check, just in case someone had broken in. She'd heard many stories about robbers who had hidden in pub toilets, only to emerge after closing time to ransack the place.

Margaret made her way downstairs in her nightie, and nudged the door open. The scene which met her eyes gave her the shock of her life. The bar and parlour of the pub were filled with strange people wearing outdated clothes. The place was lit up, and a heavy haze of cigarette smoke hung in the air. The men and women were dressed in the style of the 1950s, and all the men's hairstyles were short back and sides, slicked with oil. No one acknowledged Margaret, and she paled as the realisation hit her that the drinkers must all be ghosts.

Terrified, she slammed the door shut behind her as she bolted upstairs. Trying not to panic, she quickly telephoned her relatives to tell them about the strange apparitions downstairs. Margaret's brother and his friend arrived in no time at all and found the pub in total darkness. Margaret would only come to the window and refused to come downstairs, even though her brother assured her that the pub was empty. Still she would not budge, and so threw the keys down to her brother, who let himself in. Trying to comfort the distraught woman, he assured her that she'd had nothing more than a nightmare.

However, the same phantom stay-behind took place three nights later, and people passing the pub even reported hearing singing inside the pub. Light was seen to filter through the drawn curtains of the bar and parlour, even though Margaret had switched off all the downstairs lights. In the end, the ghosts became so rowdy, that the police were often called out by neighbours, but each time the police were always baffled to discover that there was no one at the pub. Margaret's nerves could take no more in the end and she abandoned the pub, which remains boarded up to this day.

# Curses

## The Silent Neck-Breaker

It is strange how mass hysteria can spread across communities and even an entire nation. A few years ago, for example, the local and national newspapers warned parents that tattoos impregnated with LSD were being sold to school children, when in fact the sinister tale was just an urban legend. A similar mania has recently been spreading across Delhi, in India, where there have been over a hundred sightings of the so-called Monkey Man; a strange, ape-like creature that apparently leaps about in an unusual manner and has even been known to attack people.

In 1930, in India, there was an even more terrifying wave of mass hysteria in Bombay, when three people allegedly had their necks broken and their heads twisted back-to-front by a killer, who, the rumour claimed, was invisible and silent. All three murders took place within a two-mile radius, and the killer never robbed his victims. Stranger still, he left no fingerprints or markings whatsoever.

Lord Irwin, Viceroy of India at that time, drafted in two special investigators – both were Wirral men who had quit military service during the Raj and had set themselves up in London as private detectives. They were Colonel Jim Marston – who came from Willaston, and Colonel Jonathan Hayes, who hailed from Meols.

Lord Irwin assigned the men a body of troops to track down the sinister killer who was causing widespread panic. During the first week after their arrival, a man in a small cinema was found with his neck twisted by almost 180 degrees. When the Charlie Chaplin film had ended and the lights went up, the place was filled with horrified screams. The man's eyes were staring directly at the person sitting behind him to the left. The killer had evidently struck in the middle of the audience without making a sound. Colonel Marston examined the crime scene and established that there were no grids or trap doors in the building. He was truly baffled. His friend Colonel Hayes later received an anonymous letter warning him to return to England. The letter said that a black magician named Jadu was killing people who had ransacked his home and sold the secrets of his magic to a British major. The letter ended, warning that three more deaths would follow and that the two colonels would also be killed if they didn't return.

Two days later, a street juggler allegedly dropped dead in front of scores of witnesses as something appeared to twist and snap his neck. Two witnesses claimed that they saw a shadowy outline of a man running away after the attack. Marston and Heyes tried to track down the assailant to a place called Thana, just north of Bombay. The chase continued with bloodhounds into an area of jungle, and this was where Colonel Jim Marston had a terrifying encounter with the apparently superhuman killer. The troops camped for the night in the jungle, and four guards were put around the tents of the British investigators. At 3am, Colonel Marston woke up and realised that someone had him in a headlock. A hand was clamped over his face, and he felt dizzy from the pressure of the vice-like grip. Someone was turning his head. Someone with immense strength. The Colonel fought against his attacker in an attempt to resist the twist, but his chin was soon touching his right shoulder, and still his head was turning. On the sheets of the tent, the Colonel could see the shadows of the guards standing outside, yet they didn't even know he was being slowly killed.

Colonel Marston had resigned himself to a painful, slow death in those terrifying moments, but, without warning, the person, or force, suddenly stopped twisting his neck. A foreign-sounding voice then uttered the words: "Tell Major Sterling to return what was stolen from me, or I'll also take his life."

Then the mysterious assailant pressed down hard into Colonel Marston's clavicle, viciously squeezing into his neck. In a second he blacked out. He slowly regained consciousness, and contacted Major Sterling immediately, who was stationed in Malegoon. Sterling admitted that he had obtained certain paraphernalia from a fakir, but that it was no longer in his possession, as he had sent it to England.

Three mysterious killings were soon to follow, and Major Sterling became increasingly concerned for his safety, so he asked for a transfer to Palestine, and was soon stationed there with responsibility for dealing with the riots which were going on at the time.

However, a curious thing happened some time later. Major Sterling was driving through the desert with an officer, when their vehicle suddenly broke down. The men clambered out of the jeep and, unable to mend the problem, set off to walk the four long miles back to base. As the officers walked, a number of Arabs looked on in disbelief as something indistinguishable surfaced over a sand dune and headed directly for Major Sterling and his accompanying officer. Much to the onlookers' incomprehension, the moving predator chasing the officers was actually a bed of snakes – a writhing mass of about eight to ten large venomous snakes, including enormous Palestinian vipers and desert cobras. Major Sterling fired his pistol wildly at the repulsive reptiles and tried to run away, but the snakes homed in on him.

The lifeless bodies of the Major and his officer were found later that day. The Arabs regarded the unusually determined snake attack as the work of the so-called djinn, or evil desert demons, but some thought that the black magic of the Indian magician, Jadu, had claimed their lives.

~

Many years later, in 1950, Colonel Marston was enjoying his retirement at his Parkgate home. One afternoon, he related his strange tale about the silent neck-breaker to his sister-in-law and her friends, who were captivated by the awful incidents. As he described the final two deaths, everybody present suddenly heard the brief but distinct sound of pipe music. They all agreed that it sounded uncannily like a snake charmer's music …

# The One-Armed Bandit

At a certain well-known Wirral pub, there is an old one-armed bandit with a lever on the side. This distinctive-looking gambling machine has been in use at the pub for ten years now. It was originally in a pub at Blackpool, but the landlord had got rid of it because he maintained that it was cursed.

The story goes that a man had been feeding the machine with coins one particular night. He was certain that he was about to win the jackpot, when the landlord suddenly announced that the pub was closing. The gambler was furious, because he knew there was going to be a stay-behind at the pub, and all the landlord's friends and cronies would be allowed to continue drinking. The gambler was certain that the one-armed bandit would spill its jackpot, but the landlord was insistent and pushed the man out of the pub. The disgruntled gambler was enraged. He cried out that he was a man of Romany descent, and that he would put a curse on the machine. Whoever won the jackpot of £500 would never live to spend it, he warned.

The landlord slammed the door in the so-called gypsy's face. Moments later, his brother-in-law, Kenny, fed a few coins into the accursed machine and pulled the lever. The machine lit up and began to buzz loudly. He had hit the jackpot! Kenny and his wife were ecstatic about the win, and Kenny promised her that he would use the winnings to buy a second-hand car.

However, on the following day, Kenny was drinking at the pub again, when a violent brawl broke out between two men. The fighting grew out of hand, and Kenny intervened and tried to push the men away from one another. During the angry conflict, one of the men stumbled, stabbing Kenny through the chest. The blade severed a major artery and Kenny rapidly bled to death before medical help arrived, his body slumped at the foot of the one-armed bandit.

The landlord was deeply shocked by his brother-in-law's death and was not the only one who remembered the curse which the gypsy had put on the machine. He tried to convince himself that the fatality had just been a dark coincidence. However, a few months later, a woman won the jackpot on the one-armed bandit, and sure enough, after just one week, it was reported that she had died in the Zeebrugge ferry disaster. She had been one of the passengers on the fated ship, *Herald of Free Enterprise*.

Still there were some who dismissed the two deaths as pure coincidence, but it was said that the next three people who won the jackpot on the accursed one-armed bandit also died within days of their win. The landlord of the Blackpool pub eventually sent the machine back to the dealer, and was shocked years later to come upon the same one-armed bandit installed at a pub in Wirral. When questioned, the landlord of the pub said that, yes, two people who had won the jackpot had died shortly afterwards, but the deaths had to be nothing more than coincidence, surely?

Anyway, that jinxed one-armed bandit is still in use, so if you happen to play on it, just consider that you might be gambling with your life.

# McGee's Mirror

Since ancient times, mirrors have been used by magicians and sorcerers, not just for creating illusions and tricks, but also because the looking glass has always had dark associations with vanity and the Devil. In the world of the occult there is a type of mirror which only the most brave and accomplished master of Black Magic will attempt to use, and this is a tool of divination called McGee's Mirror, which was developed by an obscure seventeenth century Irish astrologer and occultist. These mirrors are made from polished black obsidian, and they don't return a reflection like a normal mirror. Instead, they reflect strange patterns. They say that if you burn a candle on either side of these black mirrors, after midnight, you can summon up the image of any dead person. Many years ago, in Liverpool, a McGee's Mirror turned up at a certain second-hand shop in Rodney Street. Today, a café stands on the spot where this shop once stood.

In 1978, Matthew, a student at Mabel Fletcher's College, left his flat in Birkenhead and boarded a ferry over to Liverpool, intending to visit Robin, a college friend who had a bedsit on Penny Lane. After window shopping in the city centre, Matthew strolled up Mount Pleasant and turned into Rodney Street. As he walked along, he passed the window of Olivier's Antiques, when something caught his eye. He stopped and peered through the window and saw a strange dark mirror next to an old violin. Matthew read a lot of Colin Wilson and Alister Crowley books, and he immediately recognised the looking glass for what it was; a McGee's Mirror. He paid £13 for it, because it was genuine obsidian.

Matthew took the weird mirror to Robin's bedsit on Penny Lane, and explained what it was. Robin was very nervous, and advised his friend to throw the mirror away. Matthew called him a coward and persuaded him to hang the blankets of his bed over the drawn curtains of the room, plunging the bedsit into complete darkness. Matthew lit two candles and put them on each side of the mirror. He uttered several strange words that were incomprehensible to Robin, then kept repeating the word "Hitler" over and over again. Robin started to worry about his friend, because he kept chanting the name and staring at the jet-black mirror. Then, suddenly, a face faintly appeared. It was a haggard looking face, and it resembled Hitler, but he looked older than the photographs of him with which most people are familiar. Robin felt light-headed when he saw the ghostly face appear. The eyes of the face kept rolling upwards and the mouth was opening and closing, as if the apparition was trying to speak.

"Listen," Matthew whispered.

The two young men could hear the faint sounds of someone speaking in German. Robin trembled, and rushed to the light-switch. He clicked on the light and the apparition instantly vanished. Matthew was furious. Robin could speak German and explained that he had panicked because he had heard the guttural-voiced apparition of Adolf Hitler ask: "Why have you summoned me?"

Robin refused to allow any more occult-dabbling to go on in his bedsit, and Matthew soon left and took the mirror home with him to Birkenhead. A few weeks later, the two students met up at The Old Colonial public house near Birkenhead's Hamilton Square. They usually looked forward to the quiz that was held at the pub later in the evening, and Robin boasted that he had memorised pages of sporting records, but Matthew quickly turned the topic of conversation to the supernatural. He excitedly told Robin that he had been scrying with the obsidian looking glass, and that he had seen the faces of such notable historic celebrities as Marie Antoinette, Henry VIII and Abraham Lincoln. He maintained that he had even conjured up his idol, Marc Bolan, who had perished in a car crash a year before.

Robin listened to his friend's manic ramblings for a while, but eventually lost patience.

"You've gone too far this time, Matthew. Please get rid of that disgusting mirror."

"Why?" Matthew asked, disappointed by his friend's attitude.

"You're meddling with things you know nothing about," said Robin, "and you could end up losing your sanity, or even your life."

His words of warning fell on deaf ears. Matthew's personality seemed to have changed since he'd started meddling with the black looking glass. He had developed an unhealthy interest in the occult and all things sinister. He suddenly announced that he was going home, and as he was heading for the door of the pub, he turned and snarled at his friend, "Now I know why Adam chose forbidden knowledge."

A few days later, Matthew met up with Robin in the college canteen. Matthew looked as white as a sheet. Concerned, Robin asked him what was wrong. Matthew was shakey as he explained to Robin that since he had started messing about with the mirror, he had seen the face of nine living people, and one by one they had died over the last six weeks. Two of his cousins in Surrey had died in a car crash, his brother-in-law had been found dead in his car, with the engine running and a hose pipe leading from the exhaust into the vehicle. Nine people had died altogether, and Matthew had clearly seen all their faces in the mirror beforehand. On each occasion the reflection of the face had turned into a grotesque skull.

Matthew trembled. Then, after a long pause, he said that he had been shocked to see his own face appear in the mirror last night. He had watched in horror as his face had gradually metamorphosed into a skull. Matthew had asked the mirror how he would die, and the smiling face of a white-haired man had appeared. Matthew had never seen this man before. The student grew so scared that he decided to return to Surrey to stay with his family.

About a week later, Robin received a harrowing letter from his troubled friend. In the letter, he described how he had seen a man with white hair walking down the street near his parent's home. Matthew had been so disturbed that he had asked his parents who the man was, and they had told him he was a surgeon at the local hospital.

Robin wrote back to his friend and reassured him that he was just being over-anxious. After all, how could a surgeon kill him?

No letter of reply ever came, and Robin grew more and more concerned about his friend. With some trepidation he decided to telephone Matthew's parents. As he picked up the phone, he somehow knew what they were going to say, and, sure enough, they sadly told him that Matthew had died. It seemed that he had been admitted to hospital after collapsing from severe chest pains. He was treated for a suspected heart attack, and a surgeon later discovered that Matthew had a serious heart defect. He operated on him, but during the open-heart surgery, there had been complications, and Matthew had died during without regaining consciousness. His mother tried to remain calm as she passed on the terrible news, adding that the surgeon who had treated her son had only lived a few doors away.

Robin attended the funeral down in Surrey, and during his stay down there, Matthew's parents introduced Robin to the surgeon who had operated unsuccessfully on their son. The surgeon had white hair, and Robin was convinced that it must have been his face that Matthew had seen in the obsidian mirror.

I broadcast an account of this strange tale on BBC Radio Merseyside, and received numerous calls from listeners across Wirral who said that they had possessed an old obsidian mirror at one time. Perhaps the black looking glass is still in circulation then …

# A Stubborn Coffin

In 1970, James Johnson, a 59-year-old Bebington man died after suffering a cardiac arrest. Mr Johnson had once worked as a gravedigger in Liverpool, and had one abiding memory that made his stomach churn every time it came into his mind. A certain grave at a Liverpool cemetery had been affected by severe subsidence, and had also become waterlogged. Mr Johnson and a fellow gravedigger were given the unenviable task of removing the hundred-year-old coffins from the grave. I won't go into all the gruesome details, but one body was visible through the rotted coffin lid, and earthworms and several species of deep-boring insects were living off the badly decomposed cadaver. James Johnson was violently sick when he beheld the ghastly sight. That night he solemnly told his wife that she should cremate him if he should die before her. His wife Phyllis was deeply religious and muttered that cremation was un-Christian. On Judgement Day, she lectured, the dead were supposed to rise from their graves, but how could he be resurrected if he was just a pile of ashes?

"Well, what about people who die in fires, or soldiers in wars who are blown to smithereens, love?" James asked, annoyed by his wife's reluctance to listen to his point of view.

"That's different," said Phyllis emphatically, ignoring the logic of his argument.

When James began to suffer terrible chest pains during the Christmas of 1969, he told his wife that he felt the end was in sight. She assured him that it was probably nothing more than indigestion, but he started to talk morbidly about his own funeral arrangements. Again, he told his wife he wanted to be cremated after death, his tone growing deadly serious.

"Don't put me in the ground, love, or I swear, I'll come back and haunt you."

Phyllis shuddered at his macabre threat.

Mr Johnson's morbid predictions came to pass and, in January 1970, after he had died, his wife decided, against his wishes, to bury him – she just could not bring herself to have him cremated. She had her late husband brought home, and laid in an open coffin of expensive rosewood in the front parlour. When the deceased's best friend, Arthur, saw this, he couldn't help but remark: "He'd go mad if he saw all this, Phyllis. Jim wanted to go up the chimney!" he said.

Phyllis was upset by his insensitive comment and her chin quivered angrily and she burst into tears, throwing a wreath at Arthur, who ran out of the parlour to the sanctuary of his nearby home.

Days later, four men from the funeral directors arrived. They entered the parlour and fastened the lid on the coffin. The men then lifted the coffin and walked to the open door at the end of the parlour. The doorway was situated at the end of the wall in a corner, so they turned the coffin at an angle, but they still couldn't manoeuvre it out of the parlour. The mourners waited patiently outside in the cars for a while, but gradually began to wonder what was causing the delay.

The pall-bearers tried again and again, but they could not get that coffin through the door. They were about to tip it on its end, when Mrs Johnson spotted them and screamed from the hallway.

"What are you doing?" she yelled.

"We're having trouble getting the coffin through this doorway. It's the angle of the hallway wall you see, madam," replied the funeral director.

"Try using a little dignity," Mrs Johnson called, and her lips began to tremble with emotion again.

Try as they might, the coffin could not be taken through that door. The wall of the hallway beyond the parlour doorway seemed to be the main hindrance.

Suddenly, Mrs Johnson's son arrived at the house. He was a soldier who had been serving in West Germany and had just arrived home on leave, albeit a little late, because of a delayed train. When he saw the commotion and realised what was going on, he roared at his mother.

"I wrote to you and told you that Dad should not be buried!" he scowled.

"But it's what *I* want," Mrs Johnson sobbed. "I want him with us in the family grave."

"You know very well his last wishes were to be cremated," said the son, as he watched the four embarrassed men in black wrestling with the stubborn coffin.

"Mother, call this damned funeral off!" he demanded.

"I can't now," Mrs Johnson wept, trying to embrace her son.

"Oh! yes you can," he replied, shrugging her off. He glared at the funeral men. "Beat it! Go on, scram!"

The four men looked to Mrs Johnson for approval. She nodded.

"We'll cremate him as he wished then," she sighed.

When a hearse arrived the next day to take the coffin to the chapel where a requiem would be held, prior to cremation, the coffin was taken through the doorway of that parlour without any problem – nothing hindered its passage.

# Angelystor

In the summer of 1969, two 14-year-old Wirral girls, Anna and Nancy, went to stay with Anna's old Welsh grandmother, Hilda Jones, who lived in a thatched cottage in a picturesque part of Wales, about five miles south of Abergele. Anna loved her grandmother very much, but had warned Nancy that she was very strict. She giggled excitedly as she told her friend that her gran knew hundreds of ghost stories, and that she told tales around the fire in the cottage late at night.

Nancy found Anna's grandmother to be exactly as she had imagined her – an austere figure, dressed in dark, old-fashioned clothes, with a very serious manner. Although she was not unpleasant company, the woman rarely smiled.

The girls spent the first day of their two-week holiday roaming the countryside, exploring old wells, chasing colourful butterflies and soaking up the sun. One Sunday afternoon, they came across an old, Gothic-looking church, in the graveyard of which stood a gigantic yew tree. From behind this ancient tree stepped a young man of about 14 or 15 years of age. He seemed very shy, and the girls thought he was quite handsome. He had a pencil behind his ear and under his arm he carried an A3-sized sketchbook. Anna and Nancy giggled flirtatiously. They smiled a hello to the boy, who self-consciously nodded back to them. After a while he introduced himself as Rhys Davies, and he showed the girls his pencil sketches of the yew tree and the old church.

Anna was impressed by his drawings and playfully asked Rhys if he would like to sketch her and Nancy. He blushed deeply.

"What for?" he stammered.

"Just a bit of fun," laughed Anna, trying out different poses.

He eventually gave into their persuasion and agreed to sketch the girls, telling them to keep still as they sat under the tree. Rhys remarked that the tree was 3000 years old, which the girls found hard to believe. But Rhys was correct, the Yew of Llangernyw does date back to the Bronze Age. Rhys then told the girls about the church – which was built in mediaeval times. He leant in close and explained that it was haunted.

"My father says this churchyard is a very ancient place. Pagans used to come here to make sacrifices to something evil," Rhys said, pointing to two large standing stones in the churchyard.

He told how the stones were reputed to be part of a gateway to a magical, mysterious locale. The girls were still giddy and laughed dismissively at the claims. Nancy was more interested in matchmaking and told Rhys that her friend fancied him. Anna was mortified and turned a deep shade of red while denying the claim. She needn't have worried, Rhys was preoccupied with his story, and told the girls to stop moving and messing about. He leant closer to them to whisper more details about the 'thing' that appeared in the church – the sinister entity that the local villagers named Angelystor – the Recording Angel of Death.

Angelystor was a tall, lanky-looking figure with a pale, skeletal face. It wore a long black silken robe, and appeared in front of the church altar twice a year, always around the end of July and on Halloween. It was known to call out the name of all the people who were going to die in the parish. Priests had seen the terrifying apparition, as had many other members of the congregation. What was terrifying about the spectral vision was that every person mentioned by the Angel of Death, died within the space of a month.

Rhys told the fascinated girls that his aunt had seen the tall vision in black one night on 31 October, three years before. She had been a cleaner at the church and was working late, all alone in the old building. When the ghastly apparition materialised before her, it coldly said, "Those I will now name shall soon be dead."

Rhys's aunt realised immediately what the vision was and she stuffed her fingers in her ears. She was terrified and ran straight towards the church door. As she unbolted the door she heard the Angel of Death's annunciation echoing down the aisle. One of the names she heard chilled her to the bone, it was Veronica Davies – the name of her sister, Rhys Davies' mother. Just weeks later, Veronica Davies – who had apparently been in perfect health – died of a massive brain haemorrhage in her bed.

This story scared the Wirral girls, especially as they were standing so near to the haunted church. Rhys handed them the sketch he'd drawn of them, and their nerves were eased, and both smiled at the distraction. The sketch was very good and the girls were impressed with Rhys' talent. They became unsettled, however, when they saw that the Welsh boy had also started to sketch the Angel of Death, based on descriptions he'd heard from his aunt. The girls shuddered when they saw the awful image.

When they were back at the cottage, Anna mentioned Rhys's tale to her grandmother, and the old woman's face dropped and turned pale, she seemed lost in thought. She then warned the girls not to go anywhere near that church again. But the girls were fascinated and ignored her warning, and over the next few days continued to meet Rhys there. They were so taken with him that he managed to convince them to meet him at the church late one night, on 31 July – when the

Angelystor was said to put in an appearance each year. On that night, the area around the church was totally deserted. The locals kept well away from the church, and even the old priest was said to go on leave around that time.

Anna and Nancy were excited about the twilight meeting. They thought it would be a romantic adventure to meet Rhys at night, and they managed to sneak out of the cottage after Anna's grandmother had gone to bed. However, what happened that night was to give the girls a fright they would never forget.

They met Rhys at around eleven o'clock that Thursday night, on 31 July 1969. A waning moon shone low in the sky, and Rhys, Anna and Nancy were nervously whispering to each other as they approached the dark church, when a strange sound, like large stone blocks sliding against each other, made them all jump. The three of them looked at each other, their faces mirroring each other's terror. Ahead of them, was a long, black shape, about 12 feet high, surfacing from between the two standing stones. It floated silently across the churchyard and went straight through the ancient church wall. Nancy clung to Anna, trembling, and Rhys stood with his mouth open, unable to speak. Anna started to cry, she was so terrified. Then the three teenagers heard a deep, unearthly voice echoing inside the church. Only Rhys could understand the voice, because it was speaking in Welsh. His face grew ashen as he translated the words: "Those I will now name shall soon be dead."

He shuddered as he heard the first name: Rhys Hywell Davies. The boy stumbled away from the churchyard with the girls screaming behind him. All the way down the lane outside as they fled hastily away, he kept repeating in disbelief: "It said my name, it said my name."

By this stage, the girls were both hysterical. Their fear increased when they saw ahead of them, a dark figure near the exit of the lane. Anna could just make out that it was a woman, dressed in black. Much to their relief, they realised that it was Anna's grandmother. The old lady was livid. She reprimanded the girls for disobeying her and sneaking out of the cottage, and she commanded Rhys to go straight home, warning him that she would be contacting his father in the morning.

The next day, Anna and Nancy returned home to Wirral and it was a fortnight later that Anna received a letter from her grandmother, containing the awful news that young Rhys Davies had been killed in a terrible road accident in Wrexham – just as the Angelystor had predicted.

# Fate and Fortune

## Saved by a Kiss

In 1999, a couple from Moreton decided to move away to London to further their career prospects, and went to live in the Paddington area. They had been married for ten years, but they were both conscious that they were slowly drifting apart. Kim started to work from home in the London apartment, while her husband worked as a graphic artist in Bedwyn in Wiltshire. They seemed to inhabit different worlds. Every morning at 8.06am, Chris would catch the train at Paddington station which would take him to his workplace in Bedwyn, and, being such an early riser, he was usually in bed before 11pm. One evening he came home and found his wife Kim in tears. He asked her what the matter was, and she explained sadly that she loved him so much but that he didn't seem to feel the same way towards her.

"Don't be silly," Chris insisted. "What makes you say that?"

"You never hug me any more," she sighed emotionally. "You used to be so different. You just come home and eat and then go to bed."

Chris hugged his wife, he hadn't realised that things were so bad. He promised her that he would turn over a new leaf. The next evening he brought home a bottle of wine and a bunch of flowers, and a big Galaxy bar, because that was Kim's favourite chocolate. That evening the couple enjoyed a romantic, candlelit dinner. and took themselves off to bed early.

The following morning, Chris arose from his bed and left Kim sleeping. He showered and shaved and got dressed, then dashed from the house. He had to catch the 8.06am train from Paddington to Bedwyn, and he was late already.

As he hurried down the path, he suddenly heard Kim cry out behind him. He turned and saw her standing in the doorway, wearing his bathrobe. She pouted her lips, obviously wanting a kiss. Chris was in a rush. He shouted back: "I'm late, love. See you later."

He dashed off down the road. The railway station was just a few minutes away, if he ran quickly he would just make the train. However, all of a sudden, Chris looked at his watch. He thought about his wife, and how he was supposed to be paying more attention to her. Without another second's hesitation, he ran back to the house and knocked on the door. Kim answered quickly.

"Come here," Chris whispered, and he kissed her passionately, and told her that he loved her.

"You're going to be late," she giggled, delighted that he had taken her worries seriously.

"I'll jump in a taxi, don't worry," he shrugged with a smile.

But things did not run as smoothly as he had planned. He ended up waiting for ages at the busy road junction, and every taxi that passed had passengers in it. The time was two minutes past eight, and Chris began to swear as he ran towards the station. When he reached Paddington, he was furious to see that the 8.06 train was just pulling out of the station. He was a second too late. He was very angry with himself, and even more so with his wife. His mind raced with accusations; if he hadn't kissed her he would have been on that train. He dialled his boss on his mobile and explained that he would be late. Although his boss was understanding, Chris couldn't help but feel annoyed with himself; he hated being late.

He walked over to a nearby café and sat reading a newspaper, the next train would be quite a while. Suddenly, the music that had been pumping out of a tiny radio into the cramped café, was interrupted by a newsflash. The 8.06 train out of Paddington to Bedwyn had just crashed into an oncoming train from Cheltenham. The reporter explained that shocked witnesses were describing the scene of the crash as horrific. Suddenly the mobile phone in Chris's pocket rang out. It was Kim, and she was sobbing. She had just heard the terrible news bulletin on the radio too, and she had imagined the worst. Chris reassured her that he was okay. He had missed the doomed train because of her kiss.

On that fateful day, 31 people died and dozens more were injured, but Chris Browning was not among the victims, because something inside him had made him turn back home to kiss his wife.

## Hazel

In medical terms, infertility is the term applied to a couple who are unable to conceive a child after one year. This unfortunate diagnosis was given to a Heswall couple, Neville and Sandra. In 1997, Neville was referred to a urologist who ran a number of tests which revealed that he was infertile. Sandra visited a gynaecologist, and discovered that she also had problems with her womb. The professionals explained to them that the chances of their conceiving without medical treatment were very low indeed.

Sandra was very downhearted about the sad news, and decided she would think about the various fertility treatments on offer before deciding what to do. As Neville drove her home, she couldn't help bursting into tears. When Sandra's sister had died ten years ago, she had practically reared her children for her, and her brother-in-law always remarked on what a good mother she would make. Now she had been told that she would probably never experience the joy of having her own children without exhausting treatment through fertility drugs.

Weeks later, on a rainy Sunday afternoon, Neville was upstairs painting the window frames of their bedroom, while his wife stared pensively out of the living room window below, her chin resting heavily on her hand. She gazed dreamily at the flowers nodding in the rain, then grinned momentarily at the funny sight of her ginger cat, Jeffrey, taking shelter in the kennel with the old grey-faced Labrador, Rosie.

Then, suddenly, Sandra saw something that completely startled her. A little blonde girl wearing a royal blue plastic coat was standing under the hazelnut tree. She was so young that she waddled. Sandra estimated the child to be about two years of age. As the Heswall woman looked on in utter disbelief, the child toddled about unsteadily in her little red wellington boots, past the kennel were the cat and dog were sheltering, yet the animals did not even react or acknowledge the presence of the unknown toddler. The small girl then vanished behind a bush.

Sandra found herself rushing into the garden via the kitchen doors, at the same time Neville bounded down the stairs to tell his wife about the little girl he had just seen from the upstairs window. As they met beside the bush where the girl had vanished, the cat and dog raced into the house through the kitchen door.

"Thank God you saw her too," Sandra said, standing motionless in the downpour, mentally replaying her memory of the vision.

"I wonder if it was ..." Neville hesitated to use the word ghost, because he considered himself a rational man.

"A ghost?" Sandra asked.

She was less sceptical, and wondered if perhaps some child had died in the garden long ago.

"Let's get inside," said Neville, putting his arm around his wife and hurrying back into the shelter of the house.

Less than a month later, Sandra woke up one morning, went to the toilet, and was violently sick. She blamed the glass of Neville's homemade wine she'd drunk the night before, but on the following morning she awoke feeling nauseous again. While Neville was at work, Sandra took herself to the doctor – and discovered that she was pregnant.

By the time Sandra and Neville related this strange and touching tale to me, their baby had become a beautiful little six-year-old blonde-haired girl. They are convinced that, long before she was born, the apple of their eye was somehow glimpsed in that garden on that rainy afternoon, perhaps as a sign to give them hope.

Once upon a time, not so long ago, seeing a baby before its birth would have been considered witchcraft, but there are now sophisticated ultrasonic baby-scans that are detailed enough to show the face of the unborn child in the womb. Through a phenomenon that remains a mystery, Sandra and Neville somehow saw their child before she was born. Her parents named her Hazel, after the hazelnut tree where they had both beheld a preview of the child who was to be an answer to their prayers.

# Miraculous Provisions

In the early 1870s, John Caddick and his family left their crumbling, old, rat-infested house on Northumberland Street in Toxteth and moved into a lodging house in the city centre. Mr Caddick was an unskilled labourer, and was having a hard time finding work, so he decided to travel to Wirral, where he hoped to land a job on a farm. Along with him, he took his wife Martha and their two daughters, twelve-year-old Grace and five-year-old Molly. John Caddick was lucky enough to finally find work on a farm near Saughall. He received a fairly decent wage for his long hours in the fields, and with the money, he was able to rent a small cottage and support his family. Grace and Molly loved the old cottage, with its charming thatched roof and small front garden. It was much better than the crowded accommodation of the Liverpool lodging house, where they had to sleep in their clothes, or risk having them stolen by the other lodgers.

Alas, for the seemingly settled family the idyllic days at the Wirral cottage were numbered. One autumnal afternoon, without warning, Mr Caddick dropped dead in a barn from a suspected heart attack. Although she bravely struggled on for the sake of her children, without her husband's money, Mrs Caddick fell behind with the rent and eventually had to face up to the fact that she was unable to afford their lodgings. She and her daughters were soon evicted from the lovely cottage. With no alternative, the three of them decided to make the long trek back to Liverpool. They travelled miserably on foot, carrying their meagre belongings.

Halfway through the exhausting journey, Martha and her daughters came upon a meadow and decided to rest there for a while. Twigs and dry leaves were gathered and a fire was made. Mrs Caddick and her children huddled together around the flames, grateful for the warmth. It was at that moment that Molly complained that she was hungry, and a tear rolled from her mother's eye. She could see no way forward for her little family. Now they had no money to buy food, and she knew she would soon have to resort to begging again. Grace was a curious girl and, in response to her mother's obvious desperation, she earnestly remarked: "People should help us, but they walk by. Why?"

"A full belly never feels for an empty one," her mother wisely replied, staring into the flames and willing back her tears.

As the darkness drew in, the fire began to grow dim and twilight started to fall. In the closing light something caught one of the girl's eyes, and Grace suddenly pointed to something in the grass. "Mama, look," she said, grabbing the dark shape. She reached and picked up what appeared to be an old leather-bound book. It was an old Bible, and Mrs Caddick was puzzled by its presence in the meadow. She flipped through its old yellowed pages, her mind in turmoil about whether or not to put it on the fire to keep herself and her children warm. At this point in her life she was losing faith in God, yet she decided against burning the book. What then followed was very strange indeed.

Grace cradled young Molly in her arms, and Mrs Caddick closely held both her daughters.

"Shall I read a story?" she asked the sleepy children.

They both nodded wearily. Martha Caddick carefully turned the crumpled pages of the old book and settled at random on the story of Jesus feeding the five thousand people at Tabgha, by miraculously multiplying the fishes and loaves. Martha smiled, recalling how she had loved that tale when she was Molly's age, and how she really had believed that God would provide for her in her hour of need. In her mind, Martha said: "Lord, please help me and my children," and at that exact moment, there was a sudden, faint cry of a bird, somewhere above in the darkening sky. The three were startled by the sudden noise and looked up towards the sound. They could just make out a large V formation of migrating geese, flying south towards warmer climates. Just a heartbeat later, a searing flash of blinding light turned the sky electric blue for a second. Thunder followed, and the ground began to rumble and shake.

Molly and Grace could not hide their terror and began to scream. Worse still, some of the geese started to fall from the sky, landing heavily around the frightened children. The six fallen birds had been struck by lightning and now lay smouldering, instantly cooked by the incredible force of the strike. Martha and Grace were in shock, but still they gathered up the birds, dragging them over to the fading fire. The dead birds were cooked right through, and Martha hungrily tried one. The meat was tender and sweet, the taste delicious. All three heartily tucked into the veritable feast lying before them.

So it was that the poultry sustained the three hungry travellers on their arduous journey. Fed and satisfied, they went back on their way. During their journey, they passed a kind old nun who took them into a convent; there they were given food and shelter until Martha managed to find employment.

Their lives went on smoothly, and eventually, in 1877, Martha Caddick met and married a wealthy man named Charles Ingram. They emigrated to Australia and the family set up a new life. Until her dying day in 1921, Martha treasured the Bible that had seemingly brought miraculous provisions from heaven on that grim and hopeless evening.


## Girl in the Rain

In September 1965, Jim, a Wallasey businessman, was feeling a bit downhearted because his business, a small shop that sold second-hand books, wasn't doing too well. The cost of the business rates and other expenses were making it difficult to make a profit, and Jim wanted to move to a more centralised location in Birkenhead. He had seen a suitable vacant premises in the town, but the rates were much higher than in the Wallasey shop. What Jim really needed was a business partner, but he knew no one who would be prepared to go into business with him.

On this particular rainy September evening, Jim was in his second floor flat watching *Redcap*, a TV serial he enjoyed. Five minutes before the programme was due to end, the bell sounded outside the flat; someone was at the door. Jim assumed that his fiancée, Barbara, had forgotten her key, and he grumbled as he tore himself away from the television to answer the door downstairs.

Jim opened the door, and found that it was not Barbara, but an old woman. She was stooped in the shade of the doorway, holding close to her middle a battered looking wicker basket covered by a chequered cloth.

"Would you like to buy some lucky heather, sir?" the woman asked, peering in close.

Jim had a fear of the Romany people, and he quickly delved into his pockets for change, wanting her away from his doorstep with as little trouble as possible. He offered the woman two shillings, and she smiled widely as she uncovered the basket.

She picked a small bundle of heather sprigs and placed them very carefully in Jim's hand. The elderly gypsy woman's dark green eyes twinkled, and she continued to smile as she stared intently at Jim.

"You're in love, but you're in for a shock," she suddenly said. "Don't worry, dear, a child will reverse your fortunes."

As Jim pondered the strange and somewhat random remarks, the gypsy bade him goodnight and walked off into the rainy darkness. Jim slowly closed the door, then climbed the stairs to his room, dwelling on the gypsy's prediction. "What on earth did she mean about a shock, and a child reversing my fortunes?" Jim wondered. Perhaps Barbara was going to tell him that she was pregnant. Becoming a father would reverse his fortunes alright; it would be a very costly business supporting a child in Jim's present financial position.

Back in his flat, Jim switched off the television and walked to the window. He pulled back the curtains slightly and looked beyond the rain-speckled panes at the night-time street. Barbara would be coming home from work soon. Jim had bought her flowers and chocolates and a bottle of wine, it was exactly a year ago to the day that he had met her. Jim even had the candles ready on the table which he had meticulously laid for the first anniversary. His thoughts weighed heavy on his mind; if it did turn out that she was having a child, he would ask her to marry him, there was no question about it, he decided. Jim's business troubles had faded into the back of his mind as he thought of Barbara, and how he'd almost given up on love until he met her.

Suddenly, Jim noticed two figures in the shadows at the top of the street. One of them had reminded him of Barbara at first, but Jim realised it couldn't be her, as this woman was cuddling a man. The shower of rain turned into a downpour, and the couple scuttled for shelter in the nearest doorway. The man, who towered over the woman, started to kiss her passionately. Jim could not take his eyes off the couple for many minutes, wondering if the familiar-looking woman could possibly be Barbara, or whether he was just being paranoid.

Jim's trance-like stare was broken when the couple separated, and the woman began to quickly make her way down the street – straight towards the building in which Jim lived. When the realisation struck him that it was Barbara, feelings of nausea welled up in his stomach. He felt numb. He was overwhelmed by a desire to dismiss what he had just witnessed as nothing but a bad dream.

He stood, motionless, and listened as Barbara made her way up the stairs and entered the flat. She smiled weakly at Jim, but her smile was not genuine. She puckered her lips as she usually did when she arrived home late from work.

"Who is he?" Jim started, unable to contain the first of many questions beating through his mind.

Barbara looked puzzled. "Who's who?" she asked, as she shrugged her coat off and started to hang it up.

"That man you were kissing just then. Him."

Barbara froze, her body rigid. The doleful look on her face said it all. Her eyes seemed dead, as if all the love she had once had for Jim had now drained away.

"I was going to tell you, Jim," she offered quietly.

Jim shook his head and looked at the floor. He picked up the bundle of roses, and the chocolates.

"These were for you," he sighed heavily.

In the same moment, he grabbed his coat and headed straight for the door. He needed to escape, to get his head round the devastating reality that had just hit him. The bottom had fallen out of his world.

"We've got to talk, Jim!" Barbara shouted after him.

"There's nothing to say …"

Jim's barely audible reply drifted into the flat from the landing outside.

At this very same moment, in another part of Wallasey, Kelly, an old sheepdog, had escaped out of her garden through a gate which had been left open. The aged dog knew its time had come, and wanted to die alone, away from everyone. Through the pouring rain, Kelly wandered down the dark alleyways and deserted streets which she had once roamed in her youth, and tried to head for the local park. However, the weak and dying animal whined as it reached the park and found the locked gates barring its entrance.

Kelly's best human friend, a pretty little six-year-old girl named Diane, went into the garden that night in her raincoat and shouted for the dog – then she noticed the gate wide open. Diane ran out and was faced by an empty black alleyway. She hesitated, then rushed off to find Kelly, shouting her name as she went. Diane's mother hadn't yet noticed that the girl was missing. She was washing dishes as she listened to the radio in the kitchen.

Meanwhile, in a street near the park, Jim was sitting at the wheel of his car with tears streaming down his face. He couldn't get the image of Barbara in the doorway with the other man, out of his mind. It was too much to cope with. He was getting nowhere with his business ambitions, and now the only woman he had truly loved had deserted him for another man. Various other doubts and fears flooded his mind and Jim felt so overwhelmed with pain and despair that he grew convinced that the only option was to end his life. His mind raced; he would drive down to the promenade, and jump into the river. He felt so numb and drained, he doubted if he would even be able to feel the freezing waters.

Jim suddenly noticed a limping dog across the road. He saw the animal collapse on to the rain-lashed pavement and turn on to its side. Jim went over to see what was wrong with it. Its nose and face were grey, and it was obviously dying. Jim took off his jacket and covered the pathetic animal. He stroked its head and its eyes slowly closed. Jim jumped when a little girl suddenly came out of the rain and stopped a few feet away. She was sodden and shaking and burst into tears. It was Diane.

"Get up, Kelly, come on. Let's go home," she kept murmuring over and over again.

"She's gone to sleep, love," Jim whispered, trying to calm the child.

Diane's tears mingled with the rain already streaming down her face. She snivelled and asked the kind stranger if he could take Kelly home. Jim nodded and struggled to lift the dog up. He awkwardly carried Kelly to his car and placed her on the back seat, even though the animal was obviously dead. He opened the passenger door, and little Diane hopped in. Her petite face brightened as she asked, "Will she be better soon?"

"She's gone to heaven. She'll be out of pain there," Jim explained, sombrely.

Diane began to weep again. Jim felt terrible now, and took out his handkerchief. "Here, love, don't cry now," he tried to comfort her.

The girl didn't attempt to take it from his hand. It was when he looked down that Jim noticed that there were no arms in the sleeves of the girl's raincoat. He thought she was just wearing it over her shoulders without putting her arms into the coat, but when he reached over to place the handkerchief in her hand, he realised that Diane had no arms, her small hands were up near her shoulders. The child was one of the so-called Thalidomide babies. As some readers will know, in the late 1950s a drug called Thalidomide was given to pregnant women to combat morning sickness, but one of its dreadful side effects was that it caused babies to be born with terrible deformities.

Jim wiped the little girl's tears away and asked her to direct him to her home. When they finally reached the house, Diane's mother was frantic with worry. Jim wanted to help them, and he promised the woman he'd find Diane a new puppy. The next day he dropped the pet round. After the Kelly episode, Diane's mother and Jim started to meet regularly, each offering solace for the other's unfortunate circumstances, as it transpired that Diane's mother had also experienced a messy relationship, when Diane's father had deserted her and the child.

In true fairytale style, Jim ended up marrying Diane's mother, and his experiences on that rainy September night made him realise that his troubles were nothing compared to the brave little disabled girl's lot. The gypsy woman's eerie prediction had come to pass. Jim had received a shock that night – seeing Barbara in the arms of another man. Also, a child *had* come into his life – little Diane had certainly reversed his fortunes. The happy ending saw Jim and his new wife go into business as joint partners in the bookshop, making it a moderate success. Diane married many years later and now has children of her own.

## Ray of Truth

The following tale was related to me by a charming elderly lady named Esther. I have had to change some of the information, so as not to offend living descendants of people mentioned in the story.

In 1906, in Birkenhead, there lived a washerwoman called Mrs Curran, with her exceptionally beautiful daughter of 17, Fay. Every hot-blooded man noticed and admired Fay, but none could have her, because she had lost her trust in the opposite sex at the age of 13 when her uncle had sexually assaulted her. The poor girl bore a son as a result, but her mother passed the baby off as her own, so most people in the area believed that the three-year-old Henry Joseph was simply Fay's younger brother. Only the Reverend Goodlight, Mrs Curran, and an old midwife named Mrs Shaeffer knew the truth, as well as Fay's Uncle Peter, who moved to Liverpool.

I have seen a photograph of Fay in her youth, and I can understand why she attracted so many admirers. Had I lived in her time, I'd have probably been the first in line trying to win her heart. Across almost a century, her angelic face is still beguiling. In 1906, the men who competed for this angel on earth were a German-born pork butcher named Hans Schwarb, a young police constable, John Bibby, a fish dealer, Tom Lincoln, and George Duff, a greengrocer.

Of course, there were many more admirers, but the aforementioned ones were the most persistent. Of the four admirers, the one who stood the greatest chance was 27-year-old Tom Lincoln. He was tall and dark and said to have been quite handsome. Each day after his work as a fish dealer had been done, he would scrub down in a fireside tin tub and afterwards dress immaculately. He was a born romantic, who wrote a heartfelt love letter to Fay, and then left a red rose on her doorstep. Mr Lincoln couldn't write very well, but Fay found the simplicity of the letter endearing, and partly rekindled her trust in the male population.

PC Bibby was too inquisitorial and crude to appeal to the likes of the sensitive Fay. The 20-year-old constable had once cornered her in a dimly lit alleyway with well-meant intentions that were interpreted only as menace by Fay Curran. The red-headed German butcher Hans Schwarb was hindered in his attempts at wooing Fay by his basic grasp of the English language, which frustrated both him and the object of his affection.

The corpulent, round, rosy-cheeked greengrocer George Duff was friendly and comical enough, but he was hopeless at the art courtship. Some saw his lack of confidence as a confirmation of all the street gossip about him being a virgin – at the age of almost 40.

Mrs Curran wanted her daughter to settle down with a man at least ten years older than herself; a man who was in a stable occupation; a good-living man who would accept her 'shameful' history of becoming a mother at the age of 13 through an unfortunate incident that had occurred between her and a relation. In shor, a man like the Reverend Goodlight, who was only 27 years of age.

"Mother, I could never marry a man of the cloth," Fay had said in reply to the suggestion, and in jest added, "Besides, he has a hooked nose!"

One morning, a letter was posted by hand into the small dwelling where the Currans lived. The contents of the envelope were shocking. Mrs Curran took the unsigned note from the envelope and read it to her daughter:

*Dear Fay Curran,*

*I have just discovered that your so-called younger brother Henry Joseph is, in fact, your son, the offspring of an affair you had with your own Uncle. This disgraceful fact will soon be made public by yours truly.*

The words of this note had been written on brown paper; the type of paper a butcher, a fishmonger or a greengrocer might wrap his commodities in. The tan paper made Mrs Curran silently speculate as to the letter's author. Had Tom Lincoln, Georgie Duff, or Herr Schwarb written the vile letter? Perhaps because one of them was tired of rejection. It seemed that if the poison-pen letter writer could not have Fay, then he would make sure that no one could.

Fay burst into tears, and when little Henry Joseph saw her crying, he clung to her dress and became tearful too.

"Now don't you start that," Mrs Curran scolded, putting a reassuring arm around her daughter. "We'll go to the police," she told Fay.

Fay wiped her tears away and picked up her little son.

"Mother, what can the police do? The letter is only telling the truth isn't it? And what if Constable Bibby finds out?"

Mrs Curran had forgotten about him. Constable Johnny Bibby, another of Fay's admirers. Had he written the obnoxious letter because she'd rejected his advances?

"We have no one, mother," Fay sniffed and kissed Henry Joseph, who was trying to wipe a tear from his mother's cheek.

"We have the Reverend," Mrs Curran said with certainty. "We can rely on him."

That Sunday, at the church, Fay sat at the third bench from the front with her mother and Henry Joseph. All three wore their Sunday best clothes. All of the admirers were there except for Tom Lincoln. No one knew the reason for his absence.

The sermon was a thinly disguised attack on the anonymous person who had sent the odious letter to Fay's home. The Reverend Goodlight looked down from the pulpit over the black, leather-bound, Holy Bible, his angry eyes glaring at Johnny Bibby, Georgie Duff and Hans Schwarb, who were seated close to one another behind Fay, as they were every Sunday.

"Only God shall judge! Only Him!" Goodlight's voice boomed and reverberated through the church. He continued: "You may remember the story of the adulteress in the Bible, when the scribes and the Pharisees tried to make Jesus contradict the law of Moses. Jesus was in the temple when the Pharisees brought a woman to him who had been caught in the act of adultery. They said to Jesus, 'Now, in the law of Moses, we are commanded to stone her. What do you say about her?' And Jesus said, 'Let him who is without sin among you be the first to throw a stone at her!'"

Georgie Duff extracted the handkerchief from his top pocket and held it to his mouth in an effort to stifle a tickling cough.

Mrs Curran and her daughter watched the congregation closely, while little Henry Joseph gazed up at the Reverend in the pulpit, wondering why he was so high up.

Goodlight turned his gaze to the pork butcher Schwarb.

"Away they all went, the self-righteous scribes and Pharisees, leaving Jesus standing alone with the woman. Jesus said to her: 'Woman, where are they? Has no one condemned you?' The woman said: 'No one, Lord.' Jesus said to her, 'Neither do I condemn you. Go, and do not sin again.' That was two thousand years ago."

Fay started to sniffle, but the Reverend Goodlight paused, and looked down at the girl with a comforting smile. He continued his sermon:

"Yes, that was two thousand years ago, but people are still condemning other people today. Muckrakers, poison-pen letter writers, and gossip-mongers. But I say unto those people, condemn, and you also shall be condemned by God. If we all had our faults written on our foreheads, not one could call the other!"

After the sermon, the Reverend came down from the pulpit, and escorted Fay and her mother and son to his residence at the side of the church, by way of the vestry. Up in his chaste wood-panelled study, the Reverend Goodlight ushered Fay and her mother into two straight-backed chairs situated before the fireplace. He struck a match and knelt and lit the twisted newspaper tapers he'd inserted into the coals earlier that morning.

"Thanks for that wonderful sermon, Reverend," said Mrs Curran gratefully.

Henry Joseph sat on her knee, mesmerised by the flickering tongues of flame in the grate.

Fay looked around the room at the vast collection of books, then her gaze settled on an ornately framed rectangle of embroidered purple cloth, displaying words from the Bible in golden thread. Those words proclaimed:

> *I am the light of the world; he who follows Me shall not walk*
> *in the darkness, but shall have the light of life.*
> *John 8:12*

Beams of the low morning sun shining into the study bounced off the glass pane covering the framed embroidery, and the oblique ray of reflected sunlight fell on the blank open page of a large diary that was resting on the Reverend's desk, showing up the words of a letter in relief. The faint impression had been left on the page from a letter that had been written on a separate piece of paper. Fay felt a fury rise in her throat, because she could clearly make out the impressions of some of those words. She could plainly see the imprint of three words: 'Dear Fay Curran'.

Fay stood up as the Reverend rose from lighting the fire. She walked over to the desk. Her finger traced the next ghostly line of words inadvertently impressed into the diary's leaf as Mr Goodlight had written the poison pen letter:

> *I have just discovered that your so-called younger brother Henry Joseph is in*
> *fact your son, the offspring of an affair you had with your own Uncle.*

"Fay! what are you doing?" the Reverend exclaimed, realising with horror that he had been unmasked by the ray of sunlight, and he reached for the diary, attempting to close it, but Fay's angry small hand thumped down on the page.

"Mother, it was he who wrote that letter. Look!"

Fay tried to pick up the diary, but Goodlight snatched it from under her hand and clutched it protectively against his chest.

Mrs Curran put down the child and stood with a look of bafflement on her face. That expression slowly changed to one of contempt.

"Is that true – Reverend?"

Goodlight seemed frozen. He did not move or blink. For once he was stuck for words. Then suddenly, tears rolled from his eyes. He bowed his head.

"You bastard! You hypocrite!" Mrs Curran raged.

She threw a punch at him, but he intercepted her fist with his open palm. Mrs Curran laid into the Reverend with a rapid succession of punches to his chest and face.

"Mother! Mother!"

Fay had to drag her mother away. Henry Joseph, meanwhile, was screaming hysterically.

Mrs Curran and her daughter hurried from the Reverend's house and walked straight into the path of Tom Lincoln, who was supporting himself with a walking stick. He hadn't been able to attend church because he had sustained an ankle injury after tripping over his cat and falling downstairs earlier in the morning. He sensed that something was wrong, and on the following day, he confronted Fay in his shop and begged her to tell him what was the matter. Fay broke down, and Tom gently brought the girl into the back of his shop. She told him everything. How Henry Joseph was not her baby brother, but her son, and how the Reverend had cruelly threatened to expose that detail of her private life. Tom hugged the girl and said he loved her so much, and how the rape hadn't been her fault. He assured her that he would never reveal the truth to anyone, because he loved her with a devotion of which she was not aware. Offering her security and devotion, he asked her to marry him. She accepted and plans were made for a spring wedding. They would settle down to married life together with Henry Joseph. Fay's life took a much needed and well deserved turn for the better – the best man had won.

Within weeks, the Reverend Goodlight was replaced by the Reverend Hope. Mrs Curran felt certain that Goodlight had written the dreadful brown paper letter to not only mislead Fay into believing that one of her admirers was the author, but also to give him an opportunity to act as her comforter. His diabolical plan would have probably worked, only for the reflected ray of truth.

# Timeslips

## Step Back in Time

The slippery, confusing nature of time is easily demonstrated. Just ask yourself how long 'now' lasts. Is it a second? A trillionth of a second? It's impossible to define. What we call 'now' is supposed to be where the past and future meet – in the present, but modern physics says that time as we know it is just a figment of the human mind. The following incident certainly hints that the nature of time is still a mystery.

In 2001, a reader of my column in the *Merseymart* and *Star* contacted me to tell of an incredible timeslip incident that took place in Birkenhead. Martin, a 42-year-old security guard from Wavertree, was carrying out his nightly duties at a Wirral warehouse. At half-past midnight, Martin was walking through a loading bay, and closed-circuit TV cameras recorded his every step. Another guard, Frank, was watching Martin on one of the screens among the array of monitors in the TV room, when the lights suddenly dimmed. This happened at the precise moment when Martin walked through a certain doorway. The screens were disrupted by the momentary power failure and went blank. Seconds later, when the bank of monitors displayed their normal pictures again – Martin could not be found on any of them. The building was searched on foot by the other guards on duty, but Martin was nowhere to be found.

Martin, meanwhile, had found himself in a very strange place indeed. He had walked through a doorway and found himself in what could only be described as an old dark house that seemed Victorian, or perhaps Edwardian. He cautiously made his way down a flight of carpeted stairs, desperately scouring his brain for a possible explanation as to his sudden altered whereabouts. He entered a huge room whose walls were covered in plum-coloured satin wallpaper, and from whose ceilings hung large elaborate chandeliers from alabaster ceiling moulds. Dotted about were a number of expensive looking chaise-longues and ornate chairs. Lying across the couches, and sprawled upon the Persian carpets, were four or five young ladies, all unconscious, and all dressed in long, old-fashioned clothes.

Martin did not know what on earth to make of the unusual scene in which he now found himself. He noticed, out of the corner of his eye, something that resembled an opium pipe lying on the floor next to one of the sleeping girls. Suddenly, there was a giggling sound behind the transfixed guard. He turned to find four more girls standing at the top of the staircase which he had just descended. They were all smiling, and eyeing him in a very peculiar way, as if they were amused at the way he was reacting to his strange experience. A gilded Ormolu clock began chiming the hour, and Martin felt very uneasy all of a sudden. He had an intense urge to leave the eerie dwelling as soon as he could, and something told him to make his way back the same way that he had arrived. In a blind panic, he rushed up the stairs and back towards the door. As he tried to proceed, the four teasing girls came together, shoulder to shoulder, trying to bar his intended exit. The guard could tolerate the weird scene no longer and simply pushed two of the girls aside. Dashing forward, he made his way back out of the door.

He walked carefully down a long dark corridor, his mind racing after the haunting occurrence, and nervously wondered what to expect next. In seconds, he found himself back in the familiar surroundings of the warehouse. The other guards spotted Martin coming back into view on the TV monitors and went over to him, eagerly expecting an explanation for his vanishing act. Martin was visibly shaken, and stammered out his account of what had taken place. Sure that they doubted his far-fetched story, he quickly led the guards to the door of the 'hidden house'. However, when the door was opened, the gathering of expectant men only stumbled into a small cluttered storeroom. The realisation that perhaps he had just visited another time zone, a past era, gradually dawned on Martin as he stared in disbelief into the tiny storeroom.

The guard has not been able to let the unusual matter rest, and is currently researching the history of the Wirral warehouse in an effort to locate the old houses which stood on the site long ago. He is certain that he inadvertently visited one of those past dwellings on that memorable night.

## The Party Never Ends

The following weird tale took place in 1982. The time was around 5am and a low haze hung over the Mersey, which sparkled majestically in the first rays of the July morning sun. The thinning vestiges of a night fog from Liverpool Bay still lingered in the Sunday streets, and a strange stillness pervaded Wallasey's Alfred Street. Up and along that street, roamed two sisters, Amanda and Holly, aged 16 and 14, and they were in big trouble. They had stayed the night at the New Brighton house of a 20-year-old man named Stephan, and although nothing untoward had taken place, the girls had told their mother that they were staying at the home of their cousin Marie. However, Amanda had had an argument with Stephan, and he had sent the girl's packing at ten past four in the morning. Now they were walking back to their home in Seacombe, but were faced with a dilemma. Amanda had lost the latch key, and didn't like the idea of waking up her parents at five in the morning. They'd want to know why the girls were back so early, and they'd no doubt then call cousin Marie to check out what was going on. Amanda and Holly's deception would be discovered, with predictably nasty results!

So the girls wandered aimlessly about, and they came upon two snappily dressed young men, aged about 20, who were walking down Alfred Road.

"Good morning, good morning, good morning to you!" one of the men sung to the sisters.

He seemed drunk.

Amanda and Holly giggled to one another.

"Oi, do you want to come to a party?" asked the taller of the young men. He was dressed in a dark blue suit and wore a loosened cherry red tie. His slicked hair looked over-gelled, and his voluminous black quiff was reminiscent of Elvis.

The sisters sniggered again. Amanda replied, "Yeah, okay. Where is it?"

The tall young man took Amanda by the hand and his associate put his arm round Holly.

"What's your name, little sister?" he asked.

Amanda noticed that they were walking towards a three-storey house that looked grey and spectral in the waterfront mist. From that house came the faint hubbub of voices and music. As the girls got nearer, they heard a song playing on what sounded like a radio or a record player. It was a corny old song which their mother had in her record collection: *Mr Sandman* by the Chordettes.

"Do you like Pat Boone?" asked the man with his arm slung around Holly's shoulder.

Holly shrugged, and glanced nervously at her sister.

"Who was Pat Boone?" she thought to herself.

The men escorted the girls into the hall of the house. The front door was closed behind them by a third man who looked a similar age to the men who had accosted Amanda and Holly. He held a bottle of some sort of beer in his hand and smiled at the two girls.

Amanda and her sister were ushered into the parlour, where there was an old record player with loud music crackling out of it. A blonde woman stood in the corner; she was about 18 and wore outdated clothes that Amanda and Holly had only seen in the movie *Grease*. She placed another record on the rubber turntable and carefully lowered the arm of the record player over the spinning disc.

The loudspeaker boomed out *Rock Around The Clock*, by Bill Haley and the Comets, and the blonde girl started to dance in a ludicrous way. Two more men came into the parlour and started to paw at Amanda and Holly. The girls backed away, but the men pursued them, and their faces transfigured into expressions of pure hatred.

"Mandy," Holly yelped, and clutched her sister's arm.

"Get away from us!" Amanda shrieked, and ran between the men, with Holly holding tightly on to her wrist. The girls hurried out of the parlour and raced down the hallway to the front door. Just like a nightmare or a scene from a horror movie, the door wouldn't open, and the men were emerging from the parlour close behind them. One of them produced a penknife and unfolded its blade menacingly.

Holly bent down and slid the bolt off the door. Amanda wrestled with the lock and undid a catch. She managed to open the door, and she and her sister ran out into the street screaming. They heard the footsteps of the men running behind them. The frightened girls ran up the street and when they reached the front door of their home, they hammered on the door frantically.

Their bleary-eyed father opened the front door and demanded to know what all the screaming was about. Amanda and Holly rushed past him and into the living room, where they held on to each other, trembling. When their father heard about the leery men who had tried to attack his daughters, he grabbed a cricket bat and went to the house where the party was in progress. However, when he arrived at that house, he found it deserted. He had seen the house many times but did not know whether it was still inhabited. The mystery deepened when a neighbour told the girls' father that the empty old house was haunted. For many years, various different people living in Alfred Road had heard the sound of a party going on in the house, usually on a Sunday morning. Complaints about the loud revellers had even been made to the police, but every time the authorities investigated, they always discovered the house in question to be still empty, as it had been for years.

In June 2002, John, a listener to my slot on the *Billy Butler Show*, called me and told how he had lived in Wirral all his life. He related various supernatural stories about Wirral. He mentioned the 'chug chug' of the phantom train that glides unseen through New Ferry in the small hours of the morning, and he also tantalised me with an account of the strange 'man-beast' hybrid who is said to rest in Flaybrick Hill Cemetery. John then surprised me further by relating the eerie story of the party that never ends. He described in great detail how he had once been invited to a party at a house in Alfred Road by a blonde woman he had met in Victoria Place. This had happened after he had left a pub one night in 1969. The attractive blonde had said her name was Violet, and she had seemed real enough at the time.

When they arrived at the house on Alfred Road, John danced with Violet and even drank a bottle of Mackeson's stout, handed to him by one of the other party-goers. Violet had then excitedly shown him a bundle of vinyl records, and asked John if he would like her to play any particular song from the collection.

"Let's see what you've got," John had smiled, looking through the discs and reading the titles. *The Ballad of Davy Crockett* by Bill Hayes, *I'm Walking Behind You* by Eddie Fisher, to name but a few of the out-dated selection with which she presented him.

"Have you got anything by the Stones or the Beatles?" John asked, only to be met by a blank stare from Violet. She had never heard of those groups, nor had anyone else at the party.

Obviously, at that moment, John started to suspect that something was amiss in the parlour. The décor, the clothes of the people present, the records, the small talk; it all seemed so outdated. John made an excuse to leave, and was met with a sudden and abrupt silence as everyone stopped drinking, chatting and dancing. Violet switched off the record player and John left the house hurriedly. On the following morning he decided to call on Violet out of curiosity – and found that the house he'd visited the night before was completely boarded up.

Perhaps somebody out there knows the story about the ghostly party that never ends on Alfred Road. If you know anything about this fascinating haunting, please contact me via my publishers.


# Someone He Once Knew

The following bizarre story hints at two things I have long suspected: that the nature of time has nothing to do with clock-watching, and that our lives are not linear – lines stretching out from cradle to grave, but four-dimensional shapes across an unexplored continuum of existence. When Kelvin related his account to me in great detail I was very sceptical, yet something told me he was being honest. When other people backed up the story independently, I opened my mind and decided to commit the strange and touching tale to paper.

In 2002, Kelvin, a 42-year-old Bidston man, was dumped by his girlfriend Leanne. It was the end of a four-year relationship, and Kelvin took the break-up very badly. He suffered long bouts of depression, and indulged in large amounts of cannabis and alcohol in an effort to alleviate his heartache, but it was no use. Each day Kelvin found himself sinking deeper into an abyss of bleakness and despair, from which he could not extricate himself. His doctor prescribed Prozac, which had no marked effect, and his family and friends worried that he was becoming so miserable that he might try to end his life. Worse still, within weeks of the break-up with Leanne, Kelvin lost his job because of his clinical depression.

One evening, Kelvin's parents heard their troubled son chattering away in his room, apparently having a conversation with someone. When he came downstairs, his mother asked him who he had been talking to on the telephone, and Kelvin nonchalantly stated that he had been having a 'constructive chat' with someone he hadn't met for decades. The person hadn't been on the telephone, he had been in the bedroom, Kelvin told his mother. The person had gone now though, Kelvin added. His mother and father exchanged glances of concern. They decided to inform a psychiatrist, who visited Kelvin at home to interview him. The psychiatrist thought that schizophrenia seemed unlikely, as the condition was rarely observed in people over 40, and the 'loss of reality' symptoms usually lasted six months before the onset of the condition. It seemed more likely that Kelvin was simply suffering a mental breakdown that had been triggered by the emotional turmoil of the split with his long-term girlfriend. All the same, the psychiatrist asked Kelvin about the visitor in his bedroom.

"Would you like to tell me about the visitor you had in your bedroom, Kelvin?" prompted the psychiatrist, gently.

"A kid I used to know," answered Kelvin, with a toubled, introspective look in his eyes.

"A school friend?" the psychiatrist enquired.

Kelvin barely shook his head. "No, me."

The psychiatrist thought about the response and decided that Kelvin's hallucinatory child, was merely a figment of a mind fragmented by mental breakdown. The psychiatrist told Kelvin's parents that they should keep a close eye on their son's behaviour, and if his condition didn't improve over the next few weeks, they should consider having him put under psychiatric observation until a proper course of action could be formulated. The psychiatrist reassured Kelvin's parents that their son seemed to be suffering from a mild mental breakdown, and that recovery from such a condition usually took place within a month.

On the following day, Kelvin rose early and sneaked out of the house. The rising sun was peeping over the horizon as Kelvin hurried through the frosty October morning towards Bidston Hill. He gazed at his watch with the other hand thrust deeply in his pocket, hidden from the penetrating chill. It was almost eight o'clock. His younger self was due to be arriving any minute for the 30-minute scramble on the Raleigh Chopper bike they had arranged. He'd promised Kelvin junior he'd make it, and had even remembered to bring a Mars Bar and a can of Diet Coke.

One half of Kelvin's mind was saying, "You're crazy, go home and get some sleep," and the other was urging him to keep the appointment with the 13-year-old year-old version of himself from 1973.

"Hey!" came a distant cry on the icy morning breeze, along with the familiar metallic whirring of ball-bearings in a hub with a gear-chain feeding around the teeth of a cogwheel.

Kelvin turned and saw the fresh faced boy grinning from ear to ear as he hurtled down the grey road on the first designer bike for kids – the Chopper.

Young Kelvin screeched to a halt beside his future self and watched Kelvin senior reaching into his jacket pocket.

"Here," said Kelvin, handing the boy on the ultraviolet, mini-dragster bike the chocolate bar and the can of Coke.

"What's that mean, 'Diet'?" the boy inquired, gazing at the can and the unusual ring-pull tab on the lid.

His adult counterpart ignored him and started asking him a series of questions.

"Aren't you supposed to be at school today?"

"Of course, it's Tuesday," Kelvin answered, eyeing the older man up and down. "What's wrong with your hair?" he suddenly added.

"Oh! I'm bald now. I lost it," the 42-year-old explained. "Started when I was in my late twenties."

Two elderly women came down the road with three old grey-nosed dogs on leashes. They eyed Kelvin as he stood talking to the boy on the bike, and they kept looking back as they walked on.

"I told my mum about you," said the teenager, finally pulling back the ring pull of the soft drink can. "She said I should keep away from you 'cos you're probably a nut-case."

"She's right. I am a nut," said Kelvin, resignedly.

"Are you? So you're not really me at all?" said Kelvin, ringing the small dome-shaped bell on the handlebars, then swigged the Diet Coke. He immediately spat it out. "Oh my God, it tastes like poison!" he grimaced.

"Kelvin, listen to me, I have some advice for you," said the man from 2002.

The boy zipped up his parka coat and then pulled up his fur-lined hood. Kelvin thought for a few moments before he spoke. What was his advice going to be? To tell his younger self not to dance with a girl named Leanne in the year 1998, because it would end in debilitating heartache and depression in 2004? How on earth would a boy of 13 take that piece of advice? Then, maybe, the advice should concern trying harder at school. He'd worked in a supermarket stacking shelves after leaving school with no qualifications. It seemed obvious then, that Kelvin should strongly advise his 13-year-old embryonic alter ego to aim for as many CSE's as possible. He wanted to offer some career guidance to the woolly-minded boy who fed his mind on *The Beano*, *The Topper*, *Marvel* and DC Comics as well as outlandish TV shows such as *The Tomorrow People*, *Timeslip*, *Magpie*, *The Six Million Dollar Man* and *Star Trek*.

"I'd better be going," said the boy, ready to pedal off.

A tear rolled down the man's face, and he quickly wiped it away.

"My advice is – enjoy yourself," Kelvin called out, smiling sadly.

The teenager pedalled off, pulling the Sturmey Archer 3-gear stick of the Chopper into position as he careered off down the road. The boy in the parka waved back as he rounded the bend. Then he was gone. Back to a world where beds and meals were made for you, clothes were bought for you, love was forever in abundance, and every day was an adventure.

"I'm crazy," Kelvin whispered to himself as he walked along the road with his head bowed down. Had he just hallucinated that meeting with himself as a boy? Of course he had, because there was nothing in the laws of physics as we now understood them to allow such a paradox – and yet that meeting had seemed so real.

Kelvin raised his head – and saw a police car crawling towards him. It stopped, and policemen emerged from each side of the vehicle. They walked towards him. The nearest one of them spoke.

"Morning," he said.

"Morning," Kelvin replied, politely.

The policeman barred his way.

"Sir, we have just received a report that you were talking to a child on a bike on this road."

Kelvin stood there, smiling with gratitude.

"Thanks very much officer. Thank you."

The two old women with the three dogs had obviously reported the suspicious-looking meeting with the boy on the road. That meant that it hadn't all been in his mind – the boy, the meeting, it had all been real.

The policemen glanced at one another, and moved closer to Kelvin. The first asked him what exactly he was doing walking along the road at that hour and also asked him to provide his name and address. When they were satisfied that the early morning walker was not a menace to the public, Kelvin continued on his way home.

A few weeks later, Kelvin awoke one morning with the sensation of a lightened, unburdened mind. Somehow he was back to normal again. He had been through the darkest period in his life and had come through the other side of it all with his sanity intact. Without a doubt, he felt that his one-to-one with the 'ghost' of 1973 had been very therapeutic indeed. When the time was right, he decided to tell his mother about that morning meeting on Bidston Hill. He was nervous as he broached the subject and expected her to question his sanity once again. However, on this occasion, Kelvin insisted that he was boringly normal again, and he earnestly told his mother that, although it sounded inconceivable, he had actually met a teenage version of himself.

Kelvin's mother did not answer him. She seemed to go into deep thought for a while, then she in turn responded with a strange story of her own. She explained that one morning in 1973, when Kelvin was just 13, he had told his mother that he had been talking to a man who claimed he was an older version of himself. The man had been bald, and seemed very strange, young Kelvin had claimed. Kelvin's mother had remembered the incident specifically, because she had not liked the sound of this older man and at the time had warned her son not to talk to him again.

So Kelvin now had all the confirmation he needed that the meeting had taken place, and was able to move forward from that time on.

# Spiritual Encounters

## Love and Eternity

The Irby Mill public house, in Greasby's Mill Lane, had become a comfortable, welcoming refuge from the stresses of modern life to Kenneth, because the place had no juke box, no gaming machines, no televisions, or any of the other forms of electronic distraction found in most pubs nowadays. Kenneth worked in a steady office job, and each Friday at five o'clock, when his week's work came to a close, he would walk a short distance to his beery haven, where he would often lose himself in a book in a quiet corner.

Kenneth had just turned fifty, an age when many people start to survey their personal history and evaluate their life. Ken had dated many women in his time, but had always shied away from commitment. At fifty then, Kenneth was a single man, and although he tried not to let it bother him, he had a niggling fear that he would be left on the shelf for ever. One late afternoon, at 5.45pm, in the summer of 1998, Kenneth was sipping a pint of bitter, when in walked a petite woman with long auburn hair, aged about 30 to 35. To Ken's eyes she was a vision of beauty. She was accompanied by another woman of similar height with a short bob of black hair.

The dark-haired woman ordered two drinks, then she and her attractive friend looked about, deciding where to sit. They turned and looked over in the direction of Ken, sitting in the corner. He smiled, then glanced back at the pages of an old second-hand paperback edition of a Len Deighton thriller. He couldn't concentrate, and found himself reading the same page over and over again. He waited, with his eyes kept low, and hoped the red-haired beauty would sit near him. Sure enough, she did.

The two women sat themselves down at the table next to his, and the woman who had sent his heart aflutter began to talk to her friend, her voice lilting in a soft American accent. Ken risked a quick glance, and lifted his head, only to see that the redhead was already looking at him. She was eyeing him with an expression of mild curiosity, almost as if she was recognising him from somewhere. Her eyes were a stunning bright emerald, and her face was cherubic, alabaster-like and unlined. When she smiled at Ken, her eyes smiled too.

"Hi," was all Ken could timidly manage.

"Hi," said the redhead.

She looked as if she was struggling for something to say, then looked to her friend, who had also noticed Ken.

Ken wracked his brains to come up with a suitable chat-up line. What could he talk about? He could inquire about which part of the States she was from, but wouldn't that sound a bit forward, he thought.

"What's that you're reading?" the American woman asked, turning to face him after a sip of bacardi and coke.

"Oh, it's an old Len Deighton book, *Funeral in Berlin*," Ken told her, as he held up the paperback's cover.

"Oh I hate that stuff, Sixties Cold War and all that," was the redhead's abrupt response.

"What type of stuff do you read, then?" Ken asked, not wanting the conversation to end there.

"Oh I read all kinds; Anais Nin, Hunter Thompson, Kurt Vonnegut, and er, JG Ballard – he's okay. There are so many authors I'm into," she replied enthusiastically.

"Oh, very nice."

Ken had not heard of any of the writers she had named. He struggled to think of what to say next, determined to keep the conversation going. Luckily, the other girl spoke in the nick of time.

"I can't believe this weather," she sighed dreamily, in an accent that was instantly recognisable as local.

"I know," Ken said, puffing out as if he had a temperature. "You been soaking up the sun?"

The girl nodded towards her redheaded companion.

"I've been showing her around the place."

"Oh?" Ken smiled.

"She's my cousin. She's staying over here for a month," she explained.

" 'She' has a name, honey," interjected the redhead.

As the conversation unravelled, the local girl introduced herself as Cathy and her cousin as Corinne. The chatter grew earnest, and Ken started to confide in the girls about his mind-numbing nine-to-five office job. Cathy tutted, telling him that his job was high-adventure compared to hers, a receptionist at a doctor's surgery. Corinne in turn described her occupation, a poetry editor at a small publishing house in Baltimore. The most important thing that Ken gathered from the entire conversation was that, much to his delight, Corinne was single.

At 7.20pm, Cathy suddenly remembered that she'd arranged to visit her mother for dinner at 7.30pm, so she hastily reminded her cousin, and the girls stood up, ready to leave.

"Nice meeting you," Ken said, shaking hands with Corinne, then Cathy, and watched them walk out of the pub.

Soon afterwards he ordered a taxi to take him round to the house of his older sister, Val, and her husband Peter. Picking the right moment, while Peter was engrossed in a television programme, Ken followed his sister into the kitchen and told her about the special lady named Corinne he could not stop thinking about. Val was encouraging.

"Go for it," she urged, suggesting he should visit the pub again tomorrow at the same time, just in case the girls went in there again.

Ken took her advice. At 5pm on the next day, Ken was in the Irby Mill sitting in his usual spot in the corner of the low-ceilinged room. This time, he had bought a book by one of the authors Corinne had mentioned. It had taken him a lot of time and trouble to locate the paperback that morning at a large bookstore at Ellesmere Port. It was a slim book, entitled *Under the Glass Bell* by Anais Nin. Ken kept flipping through the pages, reading the titles of the story and a few lines here and there, but he couldn't get into the book because he kept thinking of Corinne, and continually expected her to walk into the pub. Alas, Corinne did not put in an appearance. Ken returned home by taxi that night feeling low, his melancholy mood encouraged by the lonely pints he had supped.

He returned to the pub on the following afternoon at four o'clock, this time buying himself a non-alcoholic drink. He decided he would try and remain completely sober, even though he felt the need for a bit of Dutch courage, just in case the lovely Corinne turned up. Once again he flipped through the book he had bought, his mind still elsewhere. He'd been sitting there in his corner for about ten minutes, when in walked Corinne – alone.

She smiled at him and walked straight to his table. Ken was overwhelmed, but managed to keep calm and ask her what she would like to drink. Corinne said that a glass of damson wine would be nice, and she sat herself down.

When Ken returned from the bar, Corinne turned and smiled, clutching the book by Anais Nin.

"Now, why did you bring this here?" she smirked.

"Why did you come here?" Ken countered, sitting himself down to face the American.

Corinne glanced down at the back of the paperback, "I'm not sure ..."

For the next two hours Ken and Corinne sat looking at one another, each hanging on to every sentence and glance that was exchanged, like two teenagers on a first date. At six o'clock, Ken suggested that they went for a meal. Corinne grinned in agreement. Ken took her to a restaurant that he'd passed many times on his way home from work, where he had seen other lucky couples dining out. The romance of the evening developed perfectly. By eight o'clock, Ken was holding her hand, and when they left the restaurant, they kissed in the cab that took them to Ken's home. Corinne decided she would stay overnight. She whispered that she felt as if she had always known him, and he admitted that he felt exactly the same way about her. With other men she had dated, there had always been that mandatory period of time of getting to know them, but this wasn't so with Ken. Although everything she was saying to him was perfect, Ken couldn't help but worry about the age difference between them. Corinne was only 31, but she dismissed his concerns, wistfully saying that love didn't apply to years and months; to her, his age was immaterial.

The couple sat and embraced. They talked into the small hours, holding one another in bed while they watched the waning crescent of the moon through the window.

"Ever heard of the Poe Toaster?" Corinne suddenly asked.

"No, what is it?" replied Ken.

"It's not a thing, it's a person," Corinne said with a lopsided smirk. "Each year without fail, on the night of January the nineteenth, a man in black enters a cemetery in my neighbourhood and places roses and a bottle of cognac on the grave of Edgar Allan Poe. No one knows who he is or why he pays homage to Poe, but they say he's been doing it since the nineteen forties."

Ken was surprised. Poe was one author he had heard of, unlike the other writers Corinne talked about. "Wow, Poe's buried in a graveyard near you?"

"Yes," said Corinne, "in the Old Western burying ground in Baltimore – the haunt of the Poe Toaster."

"He sounds weird," Ken remarked, as he leant over and began to kiss Corinne's ear lobe.

"I think it's romantic that someone should be so dedicated to a person, even after they have died," mused Corinne.

"If I died, would you still feel for me?" Ken asked her.

She turned and gazed directly into his eyes.

"Yes, I would."

"If you died, I think I'd like to die as well, rather than lose you to eternity," Ken whispered, beginning to feel a bit choked at the mere thought.

"That is the sweetest thing anyone has ever said to me," Corinne gulped, leaning closer to kiss him in the hush of the bedroom.

That single month of her visit soon passed, and Corinne flew back to the States, leaving a huge hole in Ken's life. Not long afterwards, Ken received a letter from her, saying she'd be visiting England again in a few months, and telling him how much she missed him already. Ken's feelings for her had been so overwhelming that before she left he had pleaded with her to marry him so they could live together in England, but Corinne just looked painfully sad as she explained to him that she had too many commitments in Baltimore at the moment.

Soon afterwards, Cathy also received a letter from Corinne. In the letter the true reason for her reluctance to commit to Ken was made plain. She had written to ask her to try and explain to Ken that she was actually married with a ten-year-old son. Cathy was shocked by how far she had taken things with Ken, and was annoyed at the suggestion of her having to do her cousin's dirty work. She wrote back and explained this, saying it wasn't her place to tell Ken any such thing, and urging Corinne to come clean and tell him the truth. Indeed, Corinne was playing a dangerous game. Corinne's husband was a jealous man with a violent streak. She had only given Ken her work address, in case he wrote to her home.

The situation was complicated. Corinne felt that she loved Ken with all of her heart; more than any man she had ever met, yet she was also committed to her family. She toyed with the idea of a trial separation from her husband, but deep down she knew that that would be a very hazardous option.

Meanwhile, on the other side of the Atlantic, Ken began to feel quite ill. He felt nauseous all the time, with a throbbing, persistent pain in his stomach. He took himself to the doctor, and was referred to a specialist at the local hospital. Extensive tests were carried out, and Ken received news that shocked him to the core. He was diagnosed with cancer of the pancreas. The disease was so advanced, the doctor sympathetically tried to explain, that nothing could be done to save him.

Ken handled the devastating news with bravery. He told no one of his illness, deciding not to even tell his sister, but one afternoon he became violently sick at work. Only then did he confide in his boss about his terminal condition.

Ken was admitted to Clatterbridge Hospital, where his condition steadily worsened. Cathy felt awful when she heard, knowing about her cousin's deception. She decided to visit Ken, who seemed lonely, every few days. Ken persistently asked about Corinne, and said that although he wouldn't be around in the future, his love for her would go on and never die. Cathy decided not to tell Corinne about Ken's condition, as she knew her cousin would be devastated.

On the last Sunday of Ken's life, he said a strange thing to Cathy. He was smiling, and Cathy surmised that it was because of the morphine they had injected into him to kill the pain.

"Cathy, Corinne is here with me. She came back to me," he smiled.

Cathy thought the dying man was hallucinating, until that night when she received a phone call from Baltimore. It was Corinne's husband, and when he spoke, he sounded choked, as if he was in tears.

"She's gone," he murmured in a low voice.

"Who has?" Cathy gripped the handset, immediately disliking the tone.

"Corinne. She crashed. Her car crashed. She's dead, Cathy. She's dead," cried Corinne's husband, and then he hung up, too choked to continue.

Cathy could not believe what she was hearing and telephoned him straight back in a state of shock. It was Corinne's mother-in-law who answered the phone and confirmed the dreadful news. It seemed that Corinne had been involved in a head-on collision with a car at a junction, and had been killed instantly.

On the following morning, Cathy was more than devastated, but she promised herself she would not let Ken down. Sadly, she made her way to Clatterbridge Hospital. Holding his bony, weakened hand, the tears rolled from her eyes as she looked at him lying there.

"Don't you cry," he said, "I'm okay now. I'm with the girl I love. Corinne's here."

Suddenly, without warning, Ken gasped his last breath. A terrible silence followed. Time seemed to stand still. Cathy ran out of the ward and told the nurses, and they came running, but there was nothing they, or anyone, could do now. Kenneth had passed away.

Later that day, Cathy bumped into Ken's sister Val, whom she had met just once. That morning Val had visited her brother and had been warned by a doctor that he did not have long to go. As Cathy tried to comfort her, Val suddenly calmed herself and said to Cathy: "I am so sorry to hear about your cousin."

Cathy was confused.

"How did you hear about her?" she queried.

"Kenneth told me this morning," Val explained. "We thought he was rambling at first because of the sedation, but he seemed quite clear."

Cathy was startled and told Val that Ken couldn't have possibly known about Corinne's death, but Val assured her that he had not only described the circumstances of the car crash, he had also claimed that Corinne was standing near his bed, waiting for him.

When Cathy left the hospital that day, she had a strange optimistic feeling that despite the double tragedy of Ken and Corinne's death, all had not been lost. Cathy sensed that the spirits of two people who had loved one another were now reunited for eternity.

## Lass from the Past

I have often wondered why people have specific phobias. Are they merely conditioned reflexes, formed when we are very young, or could they be the result of traumatic experiences from some previous existence? We are now moving into the realms of reincarnation.

When I was a child, I had an intense fear of the sea, and whenever my father took me down to the Pier Head to see the ships, I'd freeze with fear when I looked upon the waves of the Mersey. Going on the ferry made me feel very uneasy, but I was unable to say why. In my early teens I had recurring dreams of a huge ship sinking below the waves. It was always night-time in the nightmare. Years later I discovered, to my surprise, that the *Titanic* had gone down during the night, and I was sure that the ship I'd seen sticking out of the water in my dream had been the doomed liner. The dreams eventually stopped, but one day I was casually flipping through a book about the world's greatest maritime tragedy, when I saw a list of the passengers who had perished on the *Titanic*. One name made my blood freeze. It was a Richard James Slemen. He had been travelling second class, on his way to visit relatives in New Hampshire, but had sadly drowned when the *Titanic* went down. This could all be nothing more than me simply reading things into nightmares and coincidences, but sometimes I wonder.

Hypnosis has been a controversial way to recover supposedly lost or buried memories of previous lives. Without a doubt, hypnosis can uncover deeply buried information from a person's current lifetime. If I were a trained hypnotherapist, I could say to you, "Close your eyes. It is now the year 1985, on the first day of July. You've just woken up," and you'd find yourself waking to a Monday morning in the mid-1980s. You'd see everything that you'd seen on that particular day. There is nothing supernatural about this, even though hypnotism is poorly understood.

The brain surgeon Wilder Penfield discovered long ago that during surgery, when he applied a small amount of voltage to a part of a patient's brain, the patient relived certain events from his or her life that had happened years before. This proved that we never forget anything, we merely have trouble trying to access the information, rather like a librarian looking for a certain book among a billion volumes. "It'll come to me in a minute," we often remark, as we struggle to recall somebody's name, or the title of an old song. The "it's on the tip of my tongue" phenomenon is an example of a recall mechanism in the brain desperately trying to sift through the vast amount of data to retrieve a piece of trivia. Considering the sheer amount of engrams (memory traces) stored in the brain, it's a wonder we are able to retrieve any of the data we need.

If a person has lived before, could events from his or her past life be somehow stored in their mind? I am not talking about the brain, which grows from a single cell after conception, but that elusive, intangible something that mystics call the soul? There have been many recorded instances of people having unaccountable memories of lives of long ago. For example, in 1906, the Society of Psychical Research documented the intriguing case of an unnamed clergyman's daughter who recounted a life during the reign of Richard II whilst under a hypnotic trance. The girl told how she was an acquaintance of Maud, Countess of Salisbury. Her other friend was Blanche Poynings, née Mowbray. Historians sifted through the full transcript of the details provided by the clergyman's daughter, and everything she had mentioned in the trance-state was proved to be historical fact, but how the girl had gained access to the obscure information remains a mystery, unless we accept the concept of reincarnation.

The case that follows is astonishing, because it involved two reincarnated people who came together in another country. Danny Toulos, one of the apparently reincarnated people, was born and raised in Moreton, but left to live in the United States in 1994. He often returns to Wirral, and on one such visit to his hometown, he called me at Radio Merseyside to recount to me a very strange story. The bizarre tale unfolds one sweltering summer day on Topanga State Beach, Los Angeles, in 1998.

In August 1998, 32-year-old Danny Toulos took his wife Heather and two-year-old daughter Faith to the seaside. He chose Topanga State Beach, which was close to the family home near Glenview. Danny had met Heather three years previously while they had been studying at nearby Pepperdine University. It had been a case of love at first sight, and everybody envied their marriage, because, besides his beautiful daughter, Faith, all Danny lived for was Heather, and she was just as devoted to him. However, something inexplicable was to take place on Topanga Beach, which threatened to destroy Danny's marriage.

Danny was taking Faith to get a large ice cream cone on the beach, and he happened to glance at a young woman standing next to him. She wore a bikini, shades, and an olive-coloured angler's hat. This girl's mouth opened and her jaw dropped as if she was in shock. She took off her shades, leaned towards Danny, and muttered, "Matthew? It's you?"

Danny suddenly experienced an incredible and intense feeling of déjà vu. The girl seemed so familiar, he immediately asked, "How do I know you?"

"It's … it's all coming back. Oh! Matthew!" she cried, and threw her arms around Danny.

Faith and the man serving the ice cream looked on in bemusement.

"Victoria! I remember. Oh Lord!"

Danny hugged the girl and they stood there, locked in an embrace.

Peculiarly fragmented and disjointed memories of oddly-familiar people and places came flooding back to both Danny and the girl. Memories of what seemed like images of Victorian London.

"Danny? What's going on?" Heather suddenly shouted.

She came striding over to find out who exactly the girl was who so casually had her arms wrapped around her husband.

"Oh! Victoria, I've found you."

Danny seemed oblivious to Heather's presence and began to kiss the girl.

Heather Toulos was livid at the scene before her and pounded her husband on his back, eventually separating him from the unknown girl, with some difficulty.

"Who are you?" the girl asked, looking a little dishevelled.

Heather recoiled in rage at the audacity of the young woman.

"Who am I? Who the hell are you?" she spat. She then turned to Danny, who still seemed unaware of her presence. Heather looked into his eyes. "Danny, what's going on? Who is she?" she asked in a broken voice.

Little Faith started to snivel and cry, and that seemed to do the trick. Danny seemed to break out of his reverie, and he picked up his young daughter to cuddle her.

"There, there, babe!" he cooed.

"Danny!" screamed Heather, her pain turning quickly back into anger "Who … is … she?"

"Victoria, my first love," Danny replied, dreamily.

"Matthew, I love you. You're mine. You promised you'd always be mine," said Victoria.

"Danny, what on earth is going on here? Why is she calling you Matthew?"

Heather stood between her husband and Victoria in total confusion, with tears welling in her eyes.

"It's all coming back now," Danny said, smiling, with a look of wonderment in his eyes. Then he added, "Heather, I still love you, but Victoria and I have been born before. We lived in a previous life somehow, I am a little confused, but I'm starting to remember it all."

Heather was speechless. The ludicrous explanation did not placate her in any way.

Victoria stood there, longing to hold Danny, but kept looking at Heather with a puzzled look. She earnestly said to him, "You're not Danny, you're Matthew

Trueblood."

"That's it," Danny said, with an expression of realisation dawning on his face. "Trueblood. And I was going to … marry you. We lived in that place …"

"Mayfair," answered Victoria. "Oh! You remember me, my love. We were to marry in St James's Church in Piccadilly, and …" Victoria couldn't continue, because she started to weep uncontrollably.

Faith started to cry harder when she saw the girl sobbing, and tears also trickled from Danny's eyes.

"I … I remember … you died … you fell from your horse … in the park … and … and … you died."

Victoria bowed her head and took off her angler's hat. She used it to mop away the tears. Heather began to pull her husband away.

"Come on, Danny! Danny, get away from her, she's insane."

"Matthew!" Victoria cried, lurching towards him.

"Keep away from my husband, you fake, or I'm calling the police," Heather sternly warned Victoria, at the same time stroking Faith's blonde head to try and stop her crying.

"I killed myself to be with you," Danny said, and he felt a lump of sorrow swell in his throat.

"Matthew!"

Victoria rushed towards Danny, but Heather slapped the girl in the face and knocked her to the ground. She lay there on the sand, looking stunned, as she put a shakey hand up to her face.

A coastguard suddenly intervened, and Heather told him that the girl was stalking her husband. The coastguard escorted the by now hysterical Victoria from the area, and Heather pushed her confused husband towards his jeep. She sat him in the vehicle and shook him repeatedly.

"What was all that about?" she demanded.

"I don't know. I can't remember now. Please let me think," Danny said, struggling to make sense of the strange encounter.

He rubbed his forehead, as if plagued by a terrific migraine.

"Daddy!" Faith bawled, in her mother's lap, and threw her little arms round Danny's neck.

"Oh! sweetheart, it's okay now, daddy's here," said Danny, hugging and kissing his distressed little daughter.

"Who was she?" Heather asked again, desperate for some sort of explanation.

Danny answered honestly, "I don't know, Heather. I thought I remembered her, but now it's gone. It's like a half-remembered dream."

The couple and their child left the beach and headed home to Glenview. For over a month, Danny Toulos was haunted by strange dreams of a life in Victorian London. In every dream he saw the girl he had met on the beach. The girl he had for some reason, called Victoria.

Heather was very curious about the strange incident and urged Danny to visit a hypnotherapist. However, Danny refused to take such a course of action. He was very philosophical about the eerie encounter.

"Some things are better left un-remembered. I just know if I brought all those strange memories to the surface, I'd end up broken-hearted. This life today is the one that counts, not the life of yesterday."

Danny told me that a researcher who delved into the case actually discovered that a Matthew Trueblood had lived in London in the nineteenth century. He was a book illustrator who lived in Knightsbridge. What's more, Trueblood had been engaged to marry a Victoria Blakeney, who tragically died when she fell from her horse whilst out riding in Hyde Park.

## Out of His Body

The Sunday night of 5 November 1995 is a date that is etched deeply into the memory of Greasby man, Chris Smith. On that night, at 9.30pm Chris left his local pub after telling his friends that he felt unwell.

Upon reaching home, Chris opened his patio doors because he felt as if he couldn't breathe. He tried to inhale deeply but the discomfort did not ease. He noticed that the faint aroma of burning wood was wafting into his lounge from a local bonfire. Chris leant on the patio doors to close them, trying to catch his breath as he did so. He sat himself down on the sofa, and tried to cough away the uncomfortable, heavy feeling pushing down on his chest. A deep pain pierced his lungs.

"Must be coming down with flu," he thought to himself.

He got up, dimmed the lights, then returned to the sofa and sank back into it, still struggling to get his breath. He watched the orange incandescent tail of a Guy Fawkes rocket climbing into the sky, before exploding into a silver shower.

He then lowered his gaze and noticed the pallid face of the lonely old woman peering at him from between the curtains in her darkened bedroom at the back of the neighbouring house. Chris saw her peeping out of that window most nights. It was said that the spinster pensioner had become a recluse after the tragic death of her sister ten years earlier in a car crash. As Chris thought about the lonely life of the old woman, he had the sad realisation that he too could end up the same way. Chris had not bothered with dating since his divorce five years ago. Often his friends tried to encourage him to try and find someone, rather than getting himself into a rut and ending up as a hermit.

With those disconcerting thoughts weighing heavy on his mind, Chris drifted into sleep. He dreamt that some men were hammering nails into a coffin, but when he awoke, he realised that the violent knocking in his dream had been caused by someone actually hammering on the front door.

"Who is it?" Chris shouted into the hall.

There was no reply. Two dark silhouettes flitted about behind the frosted glass pane of the front door. Then came a rattling sound in the lock, as if someone was trying to pick it. Chris assumed the worst: burglars. He panicked, and tried to deter them by calling out to an imaginary friend.

"Call the police, Frank! Let the dog out as well!" he cried.

The rattling and lock-picking continued. Chris grew more on edge. Then the front door started to open, and Chris braced himself. He looked around in the dark hallway for a weapon, but could find nothing, so he clenched his hand into a fist and prepared to defend himself. A man of about fort-five years of age in a baseball cap came in first. Behind him was a policeman and a policewoman, and the two officers rushed past the man and ran straight past Chris.

"Hey, what's going on?" Chris said, following the police constables into his lounge.

He jumped when he noticed that there, on his floor, was a man lying face down. The policewoman was kneeling by him, feeling for a carotid pulse. The other police officer was talking into his radio transceiver.

Chris panicked.

"This must be a set-up," he thought to himself.

He could not understand how on earth a body could have got into his lounge. His mind raced in a blur of confusion. He turned back into the lounge, his mind in turmoil as he assumed that now he'd have to put together some sort of statement. Then he got the shock of his life. The body on the floor was unmistakably his own body. In a state of sheer shock, Chris felt faint, and the room began to spin. He blacked out.

He awoke, confused by the noise and light around him. He realised hazily that he was in a speeding ambulance. Strapped to his face was an oxygen mask.

"What happened?" he choked, looking to the paramedic.

"Take it easy, Mr Smith," the ambulance man said in a soothing voice.

Once in hospital, he was treated for aspiration pneumonia. It was a close call, and Chris had almost died, and would have done so, had it not been for the medical attention he received in time. Chris made a reasonable recovery, and once he was stable, the doctor explained to him just what had happened.

"You have a condition known as Barrett's Oesophagus," he stated.

"What does that mean, doctor?" Chris asked, still drowsy from his medication.

The doctor gently touched Chris's throat with his pen.

"The oesophagus is simply a transportation tube from the mouth to the stomach. When we swallow, what we are really doing is closing a trap door in our throat called the epiglottis. This sends food down the oesophagus and prevents food from going down the windpipe and into our lungs."

"Oh," said Chris automatically, still none the wiser.

"Now, you have a condition, which can be treated, called Barrett's Oesophagus, where the little trap door in your throat allowed some fluid into your lungs – maybe tea or coffee – and that caused the pneumonia." The doctor said, drawing a circle in the air with his hand just over Chris's bare chest to try and illustrate where the damage had been.

Chris thought back to that night when he had collapsed.

"All I remember, doc, is falling asleep on the sofa and feeling very breathless. I must have fainted, or something."

"You did. You fell off the sofa, but luckily, a neighbour saw you lying on the floor from her window and called for an ambulance," confirmed the doctor, as he filled in a form on his clipboard.

Chris was baffled for a second until he slowly realised what must have happened. The old reclusive woman that he had seen looking over from her bedroom window must have called the police. Then Chris remembered how he had witnessed the police being admitted by a man who had picked the lock. He knew the police had people on standby who were trained to open locks with a skeleton key when an emergency entry was needed, but Chris couldn't work out how he had seen the police enter his house when his body was lying prostrate in the lounge. Then the terrifying reality hit him: he must have had an out-of-body experience, like the ones that he'd read about in magazines. Over the years, hundreds of ordinary people who are near death, or who are undergoing a serious operation, report the experience of leaving their body, sometimes not even realising their flesh and blood body was inert, or even clinically dead.

Chris related his out-of-body experience to the doctor, but the medical man would not comment. He merely smiled and shrugged and left the room.

Until Chris had undergone that near-death experience, he had been an ardent atheist. However, since his brush with death, he has realised that maybe death is not the end, but a stepping stone to another phase of human development.


# Tree of Life

We depend on the world's rain forests in ways that we are only just beginning to understand. The rain forests play a significant role in maintaining weather patterns and the world's limited supply of fresh water. Of course, the natural elements and species from the rain forests are the basis of many consumer, agricultural, medical, and industrial products. Although rain forests cover less than 2 per cent of our planet's surface, they are home to more than half of all plant and animal species.

According to the non-profit-making Nature Conservancy organisation, eight million square miles of tropical rain forest originally encircled the Earth. More than half of these forests have been burned, bulldozed and destroyed. Only 3.4 million square miles remain. If deforestation continues at the current rate, scientists estimate that nearly all the tropical rainforest ecosystems will be destroyed by the year 2030. In the meantime, with the passing of each second, more than an acre of the world's rain forest disappears.

In 1971, there weren't many people in Wirral thinking about the importance of trees and how we were mistreating the Earth. Ecology and green issues had not fully entered the mass consciousness in most countries, and yet, in the Oxton area of Wirral, there lived a girl of 14 who was in love with all of nature; a girl who believed trees were important life-giving, oxygen-bearing creatures. Her name was Prudence, but she told her well-to-do parents that she preferred to be known by a name of her own choosing, which was Harmony. Harmony's bedroom wall was covered, not only with posters of pop stars, but also with charts depicting different species of trees, constellations, and a map of the Solar System. Harmony was also a frequent visitor to Ness Botanic Gardens, and she often pestered her father to take her and her school friend Sharon (christened Starshine by Harmony) to the Lake District, or Delamere Forest.

Stuck over Harmony's bed, on the blank reverse of a strip of wallpaper, she had scrawled the words to the first verse of her favourite poem, *Woodman Spare That Tree*, written by George Pope Morris in 1830:

> Woodman, spare that tree!
> Touch not a single bough!
> In youth it sheltered me,
> And I'll protect it now.
> 'Twas my forefather's hand
> That placed it near his cot:
> There, woodman, let it stand,
> Thy axe shall harm it not!

The sensitive other-worldly schoolgirl was an easy target for the school bullies, who could not understand a girl who would stop in her tracks and kneel in awe to admire a cluster of wild crimson poppies in bloom at the side of the road. What did the oddball girl find so fascinating about a morning moon that made her stand in the playground, gazing up at the pale lunar orb, oblivious to the joker tying her shoelaces together? Why did Harmony get excited each August when the Perseid meteors were due to arrive after midnight in streaks of dazzling silver across the starry skies? Normal girls had boys on their minds, but Harmony and Starshine were in love with the Northern Lights and shooting stars. Crazy, thought the mundane teenage girls in Harmony's school.

Then came the attempt to save the tree that was to later provide the dullards of the school with many mindless laughs. An old oak was scheduled to be uprooted because it was an obstacle to a new road that was to run through a stretch of greenery on the outskirts of Oxton. The removal of the old oak had been mentioned in an inch of column in the local newspaper, and no one opposed the plan. There was no environmental campaign to save the oak, but Harmony decided she would sit beneath the large tree – one of her favourite friends – on the last night of its 'life'. Starshine joined her, and the two girls sat drinking soup from a Thermos beneath the twinkling canopy of the night sky. The girls' parents were not too keen on the all-night vigil, and Starshine's 18-year-old brother Kristian checked on them several times on his moped.

As dawn broke, Harmony was hugging the tree. Tears trickled from her weary eyes. Starshine was exhausted by this stage, and longed for the cosiness of her bed. She tried to convince her friend to go home. Harmony refused, and Starshine complained about being unable to keep her eyes open.

"You're being like the disciples who fell asleep as Jesus was suffering on his last night in the Garden of Gethsemane," Harmony told her weary friend.

Starshine went home, leaving her friend alone with the condemned oak. Harmony's sobs faded to a hush as she made her way towards her house. An hour later, Starshine returned to her friend's side with a bundle of biscuits, lemonade and a blanket. Harmony embraced her and the two girls cried a little. It wasn't long before they were singing again to while away the hours. Harmony had a fine singing voice, and she sang a song that she and Starshine liked, a song that had been in the charts for a while called *You've Got A Friend*, by James Taylor. After the singing, Harmony made a morbid request to her friend.

"If I die before you, could you plant something, like an acorn?"

"Don't talk like that," said Starshine. "It's morbid."

"I have a feeling I'll never become a woman," Harmony announced bluntly.

"That's a horrible thing to say," Starshine said, and she tried to encourage her friend to sing another song as a distraction.

Harmony laughed. Agreeing she was being gloomy, she suddenly cheered up again.

"I'll probably live to be a hundred at least!"

That morning, the earthmoving and construction equipment arrived in a convoy. Despite Harmony's hysterical protestations, the tree was chain-sawed to pieces and its roots were wrenched up by the big iron shovel of a JCB.

A week later, Harmony was on her way to school when she saw a beautiful iridescent Silver Studded Blue butterfly fluttering upwards from a hedge. She knew that the butterfly had not been seen in Wirral for many years, and was entranced by its delicate beauty. She gazed at the sapphire winged creature as it rose up into the morning air, and was still staring intently at it as she walked on across the road. Starshine stood on the other side of the road – with her hands to her face.

A car turned into the road and headed straight for Harmony. The vehicle smashed into her. The sudden impact threw her back on to the pavement, where she was tossed at speed into a hedge. Her body landed heavily and lay motionless. Blood began to trickle from her nose and ears. The car came to a screeching halt at the roadside.

From across the road came terrible, piercing howls. Starshine came running across the road, her young face clearly showing signs of shock and disbelief.

"Harmony," Starshine muttered, gasping to get her words out. She knelt beside her friend, her hands trembling.

"I'm dreaming," Harmony whispered with a vague smile.

Starshine saw her friend's smashed teeth and grabbed hold of her hand. Both of Harmony's hands were shaking, but Starshine squeezed them tight.

"It's okay, Harmony," Starshine cried, with tears streaming down her face.

"Am I dreaming? I thought I might have dreamt that," Harmony murmured, as her eyes drifted, not towards her friend, but somewhere in the hedge. She squinted, as if she couldn't see properly.

"Harmony, you're going to be …" Starshine found herself too choked to speak any further, as the reality of the damage the car had done to her soul-mate hit her.

In those special, close moments, Harmony died. Those eyes that had been so full of life, so full of inquisitiveness and wonder, were devoid of any spark of consciousness – some sacred essence had gone forever.

"I love you, Harmony," Starshine cried, sobbing uncontrollably.

"She just stepped out in front of me," came a voice.

Starshine turned and saw a middle-aged man standing beside her. He was also in shock, and he had his hand pressed over his face. He looked through his splayed fingers, moving his lips without saying anything audible.

"She was my best friend," Starshine told him, and as she gazed back at her dead companion, she was oblivious to the growing crowd starting to form around her.

Three months after the tragedy, Starshine – or Sharon as she was known again – was staying at her Aunt Gretta's house in Bromborough, when the two of them heard something very strange. The old upright piano in the parlour of Gretta's house had been locked since the Second World War, and the keyboard lid had remained shut because its key had never been found. The sound of piano music emanating from the parlour, at half-past eleven at night, was therefore particularly baffling. Gretta and her niece slowly descended the stairs in their night-gowns and stood on the bottom steps, listening to the ghostly melody.

"Aunt, I know that song!" exclaimed Sharon excitedly. It was the song which Harmony had sung on the night they'd held a vigil at the oak tree: *You've Got A Friend*.

The piano suddenly stopped playing, and Gretta and Sharon cautiously entered the parlour and quickly switched on the light. There was nobody there, except for Sharon and her aunt. They glanced quickly about the room, feeling very uneasy.

"What's that?" Gretta asked, pointing to something on top of the piano.

It was an acorn. Sharon recoiled in amazement. She picked up the acorn and held it in her clenched palm. A single tear welled in her eye.

The next day, Sharon buried the acorn, not far from the spot where the old oak tree had once stood.

# The Bizarre and the Unexplained

## Parental Impostors

In 1881, there lived in Wirral a family called the Aspinalls. Jonathan and Kitty Aspinall and their beautiful three-year-old twin daughters, Rosie and Harriet, were often seen strolling round the green open spaces of Bidston Hill on a Sunday morning. In matching outfits, the twins would link each other and on each side, their parents would hold their little hands and walk along. Everyone who looked on thought the sight a most endearing one.

Kitty Aspinall was a hard-working housewife, because, although the Aspinalls were middle-class, they had no servants. Jonathan Aspinall was a taxidermist – he stuffed and prepared animals for museum exhibitions, and he also made very fine medical models to instruct trainee doctors and surgeons. Now, children are quick to notice certain physical characteristics of a person. If you have a mole on your face, they point it out and ask what it is, or if your front tooth is missing, they enquire about its whereabouts. The Aspinall twins soon noticed that half of their father's little finger was missing. He explained to his curious daughters that when he was a boy he had leaned against a mangle and his mother had turned it, and half of his little finger had been badly crushed. He had had to have it amputated.

The Aspinalls were a religious, reclusive – and eccentric family. Somewhat paranoid about the modern word, Jonathan insisted on keeping his savings hidden at home, rather than having a bank account. The couple preferred to avoid intrusion from people and had virtually no friends.

In December 1881 the couple moved down to a house in the Islington area of London, where events took a very sinister turn. One night, little Rosie and Harriet were safely in their beds. Their father came in to tuck them in and kiss them goodnight – but he unsettled them by his manner and the fact that he looked somehow strange and unfamiliar. His red hair seemed as curly as ever, yet his little finger appeared to have grown back. For some bizarre reason, half of it was not missing any more. When he whispered goodnight to the girls, his voice sounded distinctly deeper than usual, with a harder tone to it. When he roughly knocked the lights out as he sneakily left the bedroom, the twins were so unsettled by his unfamiliar ways, that they cried themselves to sleep.

The following morning, a strange, smiling woman came up to help them with their clothes. She was dressed just like their mother, and got them ready, just as their own mother used to do, but the twins were not convinced. They were again unsettled and began to cry, calling for their real mother. However, it transpired that they were to never see their mother or father ever again …

Ten years after the strange sense of unfamiliarity had struck the girls, in 1891, the twins were blossoming into beautiful young ladies. One night in April of that year, the girls were relaxing together in their bedroom, recollecting early memories, when suddenly, Harriet's face scrunched into a frown, displaying obvious bewilderment.

"Do you recall that incident about papa's little finger?" she asked her sister.

Rosie was combing her hair in front of the looking glass on the dresser, when she suddenly turned and gasped, "Why, of course!"

The two of them strained their memories to recall their early childhood. Rosie remembered the strolls through the parks, and how she would clasp her father's right hand, and she clearly recalled that half of his little finger had been missing. The twins decided something was definitely amiss. Searching for some sort of explanation, they came up with the possible idea that perhaps they had been adopted. They decided to confront their parents there and then. To their disappointment, they were laughingly told by their mother and father that of course they weren't adopted, and their suspicions were dismissed outright.

However, Harriet's mind would not rest. She had a plan.

"Don't you think it peculiar that we are not allowed into the attic?" she asked Rosie a few days later.

Her mind raced and she speculated that perhaps there were documents up there – marriage certificates, birth certificates – and perhaps even a certificate of adoption.

"But we are not allowed up there. We can't go up there because mama or papa are always present," Rosie warned.

Harriet, however, was not to be dissuaded, and put her mind to finding a way into the forbidden attic. Each Thursday afternoon their mother went to buy groceries, and she was usually gone for the better part of an hour. The only person downstairs then would be their father. Harriet cunningly sent him a bogus letter, asking him to travel across to the other side of London on an urgent call. She sat at the bureau in their dining room and wrote an anonymous letter to him, stating that if Mr Aspinall failed to call at 67 Finsbury Square at 2pm on Thursday afternoon, certain damning information would be revealed to the police.

The letter was posted, and arrived on Thursday morning. Mr Aspinall became very agitated as he read the letter. The twins smiled secretly at each other and scurried to their room to discuss their plan. At 2pm their mother told them to accompany her to help with the groceries, but the twins were a step ahead. They had been complaining of being sick all morning, and said they were too ill to go to the shops with her. Mr and Mrs Aspinall sternly told the twins to stay put in the sitting room until they returned.

As soon as the couple left, Rosie bolted the door, and she and her sister sped up to the attic. On finding it was locked, the twins searched their parents' room for the key. As it was hidden under a carpet, it took a while for the girls to discover it. Scampering back to the top of the staircase, they finally entered the dusty old attic. As they urged the heavy, awkward door open, the first thing their eyes fell upon were two articulated skeletons hanging in the far corner on two stands. The girls gasped out loud in unison. The left hand of the tall skeleton was still holding the right hand of the smaller one. They appeared to be a male and female. The girls were shocked by the grim discovery, but what frightened them most was that the right hand of the large skeleton had half of the little finger bone missing. The girls shivered with an ice cold fear. Suddenly, there was a noise behind them. Jumping at the sound, they turned, to face their so-called parents, who were looming over them angrily.

At that moment the twins realised that the two adults that had been living with them for the last nine years were not their parents at all, but impostors. The Aspinalls had returned because Mr Aspinall – or whoever he really was – had not only recognised Harriet's handwriting in the fake letter, but he had also noticed her distinctive misspelling of the word 'with', spelt as 'whith'.

Within a few panic-stricken moments of struggling and shouting, the twins found themselves overpowered and tied up.

"Who shall be the first to go, Rosie or Harriet?" the female parental impostor taunted them sinisterly, as she paced around Harriet.

The man brought over a large and dusty rope from an old chest across the room. Calmly, he explained how he was now going to be forced to hang the girls, one at a time, in turn, from the banisters. Luckily for the twins, at that moment an errand boy called at the house to deliver some groceries. In fact, he had misread the delivery address and was calling at the wrong house, but luck was on the twins' side and chance took him to their door. He heard the girls' piercing screams and was most alarmed by them. So much so, that he ran quickly to fetch a nearby policeman. Also very concerned on hearing the poor girls' wails, the policeman forced an entry into the house. He followed the cries and discovered them still bound up in the attic. The twins appeared to be safe and sound, but they were alone by this time. The two impostors had abandoned them when they realised that their game was up.

Strangely, the impostors were never traced. They had somehow fled and escaped. There was never any actual proof that the two skeletons in the attic were the twins' real parents; no murder investigation was ever launched. There was no *corpus delicti* – body of crime. DNA tests were obviously unheard of in those days, but had they been available, I think that surely they would have proved that the skeletons in the attic were of Rosie and Harriet's real parents. Why the bizarre double murder was committed remains a puzzle. Perhaps the replacement parents had killed before and were hiding behind the guise of respectable parents, or perhaps they carried out the murders to benefit from Mr Aspinall's will. We'll probably never know.

# The Satanists

On Wednesday 24 June 1891, Eliza Smith, a pretty, but very naive 16-year-old girl, arrived in Liverpool from Preston, in search of her uncle, Phillip Irvine, who lived off Everton Brow. Eliza had recently become orphaned when her father had died from heart failure, so she went to look for her Uncle Phillip in Liverpool, but there she learned, much to her disappointment, that he had gone to London on business, and hadn't left any forwarding address.

Eliza ended up walking aimlessly around Everton, and as she strolled up William Henry Street, she was spotted by an elderly man named Edgar Wright. Edgar approached Eliza and asked her why she looked so downhearted. When the girl tearfully told him that she had travelled all the way from Preston to meet her uncle, and how he'd gone to London, Mr Wright invited the girl into his home and treated her to a meal and a drink. After quizzing the distressed girl for a while, he smiled warmly and said he knew of a family in Birkenhead who were seeking a maidservant. He reassured her that the pay on offer was excellent. Eliza expressed excited interest in taking up the position, and that same day, Mr Wright accompanied her across the Mersey on the ferry. He took her to a large, sprawling mansion. It was a huge but strangely dark house situated on a slight incline. This slope was known as the Brew – a Scottish name for a slight hill.

The mansion was the home of the Morgans, a family that had come over from Wales many years before. As Eliza and Mr Wright approached the gates of the mansion, a terrific thunderstorm erupted in the skies, and torrents of rain lashed down. Forks of lightning hit the steeple of a local church, causing Eliza to scream out in terror. Mr Wright embraced the girl and took her into the grounds of the Morgans' vast home.

The head of the family was Walter Morgan, and he instantly hired Eliza Smith as a maidservant. Old Mr Wright went back to Liverpool that evening. Mrs Morgan seemed very stand-offish with Eliza, and hardly even looked at the girl. The Morgans' three daughters were also very unsociable, and they struck Eliza as sinister, they were always silent and dressed in black. Walter Morgan took Eliza into his study on the following day and asked her a series of very personal questions. Had she ever been with a boy? Eliza said she hadn't. Was she a decent, clean-living girl? Eliza replied quietly that, yes, she was. Walter smiled. "Splendid!" he beamed.

A few days later his daughters entered Eliza's little room laden with expensive clothes and accessories. They told her that she was to dress up for a ball taking place in Liverpool, to which Eliza was to accompany their father. Eliza sensed something was wrong. Something she couldn't put her finger on, but all the same she did as she was directed. The daughters dressed her in a beautiful robe, then combed and styled the young maid's hair with an ornamental rose hairpin to keep the styling in place. Strings of pearls were put around her slender neck, and one of the daughters found the right size of shoe for Eliza. Another daughter then applied a hint of rouge to her cheeks.

Eliza was bundled into a long coat with a hood and taken over to another palatial house in the Aigburth district of Liverpool. A footman helped the girl from the carriage, and ushered her into the house. Walter Morgan held her hand as they walked up a sumptuous blood-red, carpeted stairway. They were heading towards the dance hall. The party was going on in several rooms, and huge golden chandeliers hung from the elaborately decorated alabaster ceilings. Enormous potted palms were dotted about the place, and a man was playing a large grand piano in one corner. The room was crowded with guests, Eliza was captivated by the glamour of all the other finely dressed gentlemen and their ladies.

Straight away, Mr Morgan introduced Eliza to three middle-aged men. They seemed welcoming, and told the maid to take a seat, and then they pulled chairs over and sat around her. They offered her drinks, including absinthe. Within an hour of such keen persuasion, Eliza was so intoxicated that she could barely stand up. The three men smiled at her, and in what seemed like seconds, Eliza blacked out.

When she came round, she was horrified to find herself completely naked. She was lying on a long table that was covered with green velvet. As she struggled in great distress, she realised that her wrists and ankles were tied to something; she couldn't move. She looked about in horror and saw that she was surrounded by a group of men dressed in black gowns. They were all muttering incomprehensible words in something that sounded to her like Latin. Eliza could see that the three men who had been talking to her at the ball were also standing there, all now dressed in long black robes as well.

The sinister group were Satanists, and they were holding a black mass. The ritual involves a sacrifice of flesh and blood – essential to the ceremony is the body of a virgin. The dark figures closed in, and Eliza noticed that one of them held a red-headed child of about three years of age. The sweet child was passed to Walter Morgan, who was clasping a long dagger to its throat. The child seemed drugged or drunk, unaware of the terror encompassing it. In such a black mass, the child is sacrificed, and the blood splashed on to the virginal girl.

Eliza let out a terrible scream as she noticed the knife, and Mr Morgan suddenly hesitated. The three men urged him to carry out the heinous act, but he seemed to be suffering a crisis of conscience. He suddenly threatened the other Satanists with the long knife and backed out of the darkened room clutching the child. Eliza was so terrified at the thought of what lay ahead of her that she fainted. When she came to, she was confused to find that she was being quickly dressed by a woman. This woman took the girl into a hansom cab and paid the driver to drop her off miles away. Eliza was dazed, but managed to get herself to the nearest police station, where she stammered out her awful story. Unfortunately the police did not take her very seriously and only paid a single visit to Walter Morgan He dismissed the accusations, assuring the police that the maid was just "an unbalanced publicity seeker".

Nothing was ever proved, so poor Eliza had no choice but to return to Preston, where she arrived in a dreadful state.

# The Case of the Vanishing Magician

In 1959, three merchant navy men left their ship after it had docked at New York. The men were old friends: the Cornish cook, Billy Wheeler, the Scottish bosun, David MacDonald, and the ship's radio operator, Derek Quilley, from Bebington. The three of them took shore leave for a few days and blew their money in various bars around Brooklyn, where one of the men had a sweetheart.

On the last day of shore leave, Derek came up with the drunken idea that they should visit the Paramount Theatre in Brooklyn, to laugh at the terrible comedians and corny magicians that were featured in the matinees there. And so the three inebriated men staggered into the theatre.

A magician, William Neff, came on stage first. Neff was a veteran magician and a very mysterious man who had patented many tricks, including the famous Neff Miracle Rope, a special rope that seemed to join back up again after it appeared to have been cut through with scissors. Neff was also renowned for his Hollywood connections. He had attended the same high school as Jimmy Stewart, and they had even had a double magic act together many years ago. Neff was also a great friend of the Oscar-winning actor Ray Milland.

The men from the Liverpool ship did little to stifle their laughter while they watched Neff's act, but the magician was not distracted and managed to not even acknowledge their heckling jibes. For that particular performance that afternoon, there was an especially small audience of only about twenty people. At the climax of the show, Neff rolled a huge glass or perspex case on to the stage, and beckoned a man from the wings to join him onstage. The man was a small-time magician called Mr Cicero. Neff announced in a bellowing voice, which echoed around the almost empty venue:

"Ladies and gentleman, you are about to see history being made today. Without using mirrors, sleight of hand, or hypnosis, I will make a man vanish before your very eyes."

Mr Cicero, a small, balding man, stepped into the glass case, and William Neff then wheeled a huge piece of electrical apparatus on to the stage. Cables trailed from the equipment, which had various dials and switches on its panel. The magician clicked the switches, and the case lit up with a blue luminescence, very reminiscent of ultraviolet light. A loud buzzing drilled through everyone's ears in the audience, and the three sailors began to swear and protest. After about 30 seconds, William Neff threw a switch and there was silence. People gasped as they saw, right before their eyes, Mr Cicero slowly becoming transparent. They could see right through the translucent man so that the red satin travel curtain that was behind him was clearly visible. Then, just moments later, Mr Cicero had indeed vanished. William Neff turned to face his bemused audience. Slowly, he scanned the amazed faces in the audience, basking in their astonishment and obviously proud of his work. He then produced a silver fob watch from his waistcoat and inspected it, as if timing the experience.

Mr Neff counted for a moment, before then throwing another switch on the stage apparatus, and the same ear-piercing buzzing sound started again. However, the sound suddenly dropped in pitch, and there was a flash of light. Sparks showered from the machine, and smoke began to billow from it. A man rushed from the wings and examined the machine in an anxious manner. William Neff opened the glass case, and as he did so, Derek also ran to the edge of the stage, hoping to see Mr Cicero climbing up from a trap door, but when he got there, he could see that there was no trap door. Worse still, the glass case was clearly empty. William Neff hurried into the case, trying to clear the heavy smoke by waving his gloved hand about, as if he was wafting away a disagreeable odour. The magician's expression was one of total horror. In minutes, the management were in the auditorium and a formal announcement insisted that everyone was to leave the building immediately. Apologies were made and they were reassured as they were hurried out, that they would all be reimbursed for the inconvenience.

The three sailors were reluctant to go back to their ship, curious to know what had happened. Alas, they were aware of their duty and left their curiosity in the port. Soon they found themselves berthed in Liverpool, far away from the bizarre goings on of the week before. They were keen to tell people back home what they had seen, but few believed their strange tale.

However, when William Neff died in 1967, an American broadcaster, LJ Knebel, enigmatically stated that Neff had achieved invisibility but had no control over the revolutionary method of making a person or object transparent. There were also strange rumours that Neff had tried to patent a revolutionary machine that could make a person invisible, and that Neff had tested this machine on human guinea pigs in the late 1950s and early 1960s. Knebel's statement, and the odd rumours of the invisibility device, therefore seem to independently back up the bizarre tale told by the three merchant navy men.


## The Hilbre Whirlpool

Hilbre Island is actually made up of three islands known as Hilbre, Middle Eye (Little Hilbre) and Little Eye. In 1140, both Hilbre and West Kirby were owned by the Benedictine monks of St Werburgh's Abbey of Chester, up until the dissolution of the Abbey in 1540.

Bizarrely, in 1149 AD, there is a mention of a strange monster living in the sea off Hilbre Island which manifested itself as a maelstrom, or vortex, sucking under people and ships towards their doom. Tales of the giant whirlpool are now thought of as exaggerated folk tales, but funnily enough, there have been a number of reports of a strange whirlpool in the vicinity of Hilbre Island over the years.

In particular, in the summer of 1972, the Wheeler family from Frankby were enjoying a day out at Hilbre Island. They relaxed in the sunshine and total tranquillity as they walked along the coast, collecting shells and so on, when ten-year-old David Wheeler drew his dad's attention to a strange sight. About 200 yards offshore, a vigorous whirlpool could be seen. It seemed to be very powerful, and was edging into another direction, moving northwards and heading inshore. The family became concerned as they realised that a couple bobbing about on the waves in a rubber dinghy were about to be caught up in the looming whirlpool. They were rowing like mad to get away from it, but the strength of the whirlpool was too strong to resist and so they ended up diving from the dinghy and desperately swimming towards the shore. Within seconds the whirlpool had swallowed up the dinghy, which then spiralled downwards, deep beneath the waves.

Mr Wheeler was deeply disturbed by the sight, and he grabbed his son and younger daughter by the hand. The family quickly made their way south to get as far away from the destructive whirlpool as possible. They eventually settled down at a part of the coast that seemed safe enough to bathe, and David and Joanne started to paddle and play about in the shallow waters again. About 15 minutes later, David's little toy lifebelt started to tug and drift away from him. Noticing the change in current, Mr and Mrs Wheeler called to their son and daughter, beckon ing them back to safety. David turned around and noticed the awful whirlpool coming straight towards him. Like a gigantic magnet, it was pulling his lifebelt towards its gaping mouth, along with seaweed and sea foam, that was swirling into the pull of the whirlpool. David attempted to chase the lifebelt and yank it back, but his father had seen enough and ran out to his children. Grabbing both David and Joanne, he bravely pulled them on to the safety of the sands.

Five hours later, the family were still reliving the events of their unusual day. And as the tide went out, the Wheeler's decided to make their way home, travelling along Dee Lane in West Kirby.

The following Sunday, Mr Wheeler and his family were visiting relatives in Liverpool. They decided to walk along Otterspool Promenade with two other families, looking for a suitable picnic spot. David and a friend ran on ahead and made their way along the Cast Iron Shore, when they suddenly heard what could only be described as a strange, low, rumbling sound. The boys became afraid when they realised that the noise was coming from another whirlpool, which appeared about a hundred feet away from the riverbank. Dozens of passers-by also caught sight of the swirling waters. The noise it made was like an exaggerated version of the noise you hear when a bathplug is pulled out. It churned and gurgled ominously. The sound was so disturbing, that Mr Wheeler had the uncanny feeling that the whirlpool wasn't something natural – that the powerful force in the water was somehow alive.

Could it be possible that this wandering whirlpool is the same maelstrom mentioned by the Benedictine monks in the year 1149?

# Queen Victoria's Atom Bomb

The following amazing story was allegedly related in the letters page of a Bombay newspaper in the 1960s. Inquiries by various researchers at the Ministry of Defence have failed to resolve the claims, because defence officials have never confirmed or denied the astounding assertions. I personally suspect that the story of 'Queen Victoria's Atom Bomb' has its genesis in urban legend rather than solid fact, but that is only my opinion. I have decided to include the tale here because the main character – the alleged inventor of a Victorian weapon of mass destruction – hailed from Neston.

In the year 1789, the radioactive element uranium was discovered. At that time nobody dreamt that a simple chunk of metal would one day destroy an entire city. The orthodox history books would have us believe that the atom bomb was thrown together in the mid 1940s to end the war with Japan, but, believe it or not, there have been claims for many years that weapons of mass destruction were known to exist as far back as the Victorian age.

In the 1880s, several uranium mines were discovered in Cornwall. A popular legend has it that Charles Edward Clarke, a genius from Neston, had several kilograms of the unrefined uranium ore transferred to the Cavendish laboratories in Cambridge, where he was a professor working for the military. Clarke had developed a theory of nuclear fission based on the work of the scientist, Dalton, and he was decades ahead of his time. Clarke had come to the terrifying conclusion that an 'atomic bomb' – a phrase that was later popularly coined in a short story by the prophetic writer HG Wells in 1913 – could be created using about 50 pounds of refined uranium and a simple clockwork detonator. Clarke knew the radioactive materials would have to be brought together very rapidly by a controlled implosion to trigger the nuclear chain reaction. Professor Clarke is said to have told the top brass in Whitehall that his weapon would be the weapon to end all wars, and somewhere along the line, the Prime Minister, Lord Salisbury, and several military bigwigs from Sandhurst, gave Clarke a blank cheque to develop his weapon – as long as he carried out his dangerous experiments outside England. He was assigned a tract of desolate land in the Rajasthan Desert in north-west India. This was during the days of the British Empire when the United Kingdom owned vast parts of the world.

Frederick Sleigh Roberts – who was Field Marshall Lord Roberts of Kandahar – was allegedly appointed as Commander in Chief of the top secret project. No one was to know about the British troops' presence in the Rajasthan Desert – even though the soldiers wore their usual vivid scarlet tunics! The villagers from the nearby village of Pokharan eyed the clandestine proceedings with deep suspicion, and well they might.

Some fourteen months afterwards, a huge metal globe, around six feet in diameter, was carefully transported to the centre of the desert. A clockwork detonator with a 90-minute fuse was cranked and activated, and the troops retreated to an observation trench almost ten miles away. Several people in the village of Pokharan, 15 miles away, were probably blinded by the groundburst explosion. The detonation was described by Field Marshall Roberts as 'Biblical' in its proportions. The mushroom cloud ballooned over the desert, giving the world a glimpse of the nuclear symbol that would haunt every country in the following centuries. The ground shook, the terrified horses in the military compound whinnied, wide-eyed with terror, and some broke their tethers and ran off.

Through smoked glass, Charles Edward Clarke watched as the rising fireball of miniature, artificial sun scorched several square miles of desert, before then punching a hole in the clouds as it rose up into space. A hurricane of heated air swept through the camp, followed by a blinding sandstorm. Lightning flashed down from the column of dust rising in the desert chaos, and one of the observation trenches collapsed through the ground-quake, burying several spectators. Because of their curiosity, a number of troops who had been warned not to look at the atomic fireball were blinded for life by its searing super-luminous rays.

Field Marshall Roberts was left speechless by the awesome spectacle, and later urged his superiors at Sandhurst to shelve the apocalyptic bomb on the grounds that it was simply too destructive to ever be used. In a way, this would be the first recorded instance of someone wanting to 'ban the bomb'. After a long feasibility study, the Victorian atom bomb was deemed impractical, as there was no effective way to place it in the midst of the enemy. Someone suggested dropping it from a balloon, but that wouldn't have worked. Zeppelins would have been no use either, as the bomb was simply too heavy and cumbersome. It seems that Clarke's crazy weapon of mass destruction was filed away in the same vault that held the early patents of Babbage's computer, guided rockets, and other inventions that were ahead of their time. The early atom bomb was forgotten, perhaps until the 1930s. And that is where our historical urban legend ends – or does it?

In 1974, India decided to use the Rajasthan Desert to detonate its own atom bomb, and found out that the site had a huge crater which was too recent to have been made by a meteor. The area was also mildly radioactive. Is this proof that Clarke's bomb actually existed? We may know more one day.

It is sobering to imagine how the course of modern history would have turned out if atom bombs had been used in the First World War. Even more chilling; imagine if Hitler had somehow come into possession of atomic weaponry!

# The Ship on the Mountain

In 1935, David King, from Bromborough, lay near to death in a jail in an obscure village in southern France called Lavardac. He had been imprisoned for stabbing a man in the arm during a drunken brawl. King repeatedly proclaimed his innocence, insisting that the injury had been inflicted in self-defence. A French writer, Samuel Viteau, was in the same jail, researching a book on crime and punishment, when Mr King invited him into his small cell. King confided in him an outlandish story, which was allegedly later substantiated by other people. What follows is a summary of the astounding tale that King told Viteau.

After World War One, David King became mentally unbalanced as a result of the horrors he had witnessed in the trenches. Against orders, he refused to return home with his regiment, and instead fled into the French countryside. There, King met and befriended French aviator and ex-flying ace, Zeno Juvenal. Juvenal had captured a German Albatross 2 reconnaissance biplane that he had nicknamed 'The Flying Dutchman'. The biplane, which had two synchronised Spandau machine guns, had two seats, and in this aircraft, Juvenal and King became nomadic wanderers of the skies, flying across Europe in search of adventure.

Unfortunately, Juvenal was extremely fond of his wine and would often drink from the bottle as he flew the biplane. A reckless character, he would often hurl the empty wine bottle from 10,000 feet. On one occasion, Juvenal slumped into a drunken snooze while still at the controls, and King had to fire his pistol to wake him, whilst on another occasion, while flying over Italy, the Frenchman drunkenly opened fire with the Spandaus in reaction to a child's kite. Juvenal had panicked and imagined the kite to be von Richtofen. These madcap incidents illustrated the mental condition of the eccentric Frenchman. In conjunction with Juvenal's carefree risk-taking, David King had an equally strong suicidal streak. With a darkly cynical perspective on life, he was resigned to the assumption that he would perish in the Flying Dutchman sooner or later.

In the spring of 1921, the two idiots of the air flouted international law and completely violated the airspace of five countries, including Greece and Turkey. One British biplane made the mistake of chasing Juvenal's plane, and the French pilot performed a suicidal loop and peppered the British plane's fuselage with bullet-holes. Realising that the attacking pilot was obviously a flying ace, the pilot of the British plane dived out of harm's way and managed to land his damaged plane intact.

Juvenal was in the habit of draining the fuel tank of his plane by flying non-stop for an hour; his erratic philosophy also dismissed the use of maps. In April 1921, Juvenal felt his mind succumbing to travel fatigue, so he performed a sudden landing in north-eastern Turkey, and it was there that he and King made an earth-shattering discovery.

Juvenal and King decided to leave the battered old biplane to explore the area in which they had landed. They found themselves on a high plain below a mountain, and went in search of a village where they could find somewhere to eat and drink, but they drew a blank. Then David King noticed something very strange. A huge pointed stone, about 18 feet in height and resembling a giant needle, was protruding out of the hillside. At the top of the stone, there was an oval-shaped hole. His bumbling companion suddenly called out "Mon Dieu!" as he gazed through his collapsible brass telescope. King threw his head back and gazed up at the mountain, and he too saw something incredible. Before them was a gigantic wooden structure, at least 400 feet in length. It lay embedded in the immense layers of snow, halfway up the mountain. The giant frame was like a ship with a wooden hull, only it was the size of the *Lusitania*. Both men were confused as to how a colossal ship could possibly have found its way up a mountain.

David King and Zeno Juvenal turned to look at one another, and both knew what the other was thinking. Could the impressive wooden structure be the remains of Noah's Ark? David then looked at the huge stone with the hole in the top, and wondered if that had been the anchor of the biblical ship.

"Do you realise what we might have found, Juvenal?" King asked in a whisper.

The Frenchman simply smiled. They both started scrambling up the steep rocks as quickly as they could, towards what was possibly to become the most important archaeological discovery of the last 4000 years, towards the great ship that was mentioned in Genesis.

"We'll be rich, Mr King," the Frenchman said, punching the air with a cheer that echoed off the sides of the vast mountain.

King laughed.

"We'll be rich and famous, and we'll go down in history!"

The Frenchman screamed with joy, and took his pistol from its holster and discharged a volley of shots into the wide open sky, until the barrel clicked empty. King laughed, and the two men started to clamber faster and faster up the mountain.

Within a fraction of a second the men's joy had turned to horror, as they heard a deep, ominous rumble which they could feel beneath their feet. The six pistol shots had triggered an avalanche! Enormous slabs of snow, which had been loosened by the spring thaw, had broken away and started to cascade down the mountainside, surrounded by a deadly cloud. Tons and tons of ice and compacted snow bore down on the two adventurers, gathering momentum with each passing second. The icy mass engulfed the gargantuan vessel, burying more than half of it.

"Run!" King shrieked.

"We'll never make it," the Frenchman shouted, although he turned, and he too made a desperate dash for the biplane.

Juvenal threw himself into the seat, while King ran to the propeller and tried to push it round to start the engine. Juvenal screamed at him to hurry up, but the temperature was affecting the engine. King tried once more, and when he looked up, he saw Juvenal kissing the rosary beads which he carried round his neck. He shook his head as the avalanche roared from behind, travelling at hundreds of miles per hour. It smashed the plane as if it was a moth, and the two men and the biplane were thrown down the mountainside.

King awoke to find himself in a tiny room, attended by several Turkish officials. His legs had both been broken, and an interpreter told him he had been extremely lucky to survive the avalanche. His friend's body had been found in the mangled wreckage of the plane. He had been killed instantly. King drowsily tried to tell his rescuers and the Turkish officials about his vision of the Ark, but his ramblings were ignored, put down to drug induced delirium.

He later discovered that the avalanche had taken place on Mount Ararat. Once he was well enough to leave hospital, the Turkish officials banished King from the country, and he had the impression that they knew about the existence of Noah's ship.

Shortly after relating this amazing tale, David King died in prison. Was he just a spinner of yarns, or did a Frenchman and a man from Wirral once locate Noah's Ark on that remote Turkish mountainside?

## A Knight's Tale

In 1811, Edward Lightfoot, a Pensby farmer, arrived at his elder brother Cuthbert's home at Stoney Meadow farm in the hamlet of Bowscombe, on the Isle of Wight, accompanied by his heavily-pregnant wife Anne. The couple had come to the farm at Cuthbert's request, because he was dying of consumptive lung disease. Days after Edward's arrival, Cuthbert passed away in his sleep, and Edward inherited the farm. The farm at Pensby was left in the hands of Edward's cousin, a young man named Hargreaves. Now Edward Lightfoot had the daunting task of handling a much larger farm, and was helped by a kindly neighbouring farmer, George Brewster.

On the day of Cuthbert Lightfoot's funeral, Edward's wife went into labour, and is said to have given birth to a baby girl in the church. The baby was named Lucy. She had a beautiful elfin face and a crown of healthy black hair. It was acknowledged throughout Bowscombe that she was the most beautiful girl in the village.

At the age of 12, Lucy displayed a remarkable natural talent for riding a horse that seemed well in advance of her years. It was at this age that she worried her parents by suddenly claiming that she had memories of a previous life. She often claimed to have been the wife of a prominent knight who had fought in the Crusades. One day, in her early teens, Lucy came across a book about King Arthur. She was fascinated by the legends and spent days in her room reading the thrilling romantic narratives about the legendary ruler of the Britons and his loyal Knights of the Round Table.

Around the age of 15, Lucy suddenly rode out of Bowscombe and made her way to the parish of Gatcombe, to the 13th century church of St Olave. This church had been built by the Estur family, descendants of one of the three knights to whom William I granted the lands of the Isle of Wight in 1086. In the chancel of St Olave's there is a carved oaken figure of a recumbent knight who holds a short sword called a misericord, a long-bladed dagger that was given to an injured or dying adversary, so he could put himself out of his misery. The misericord was not a wooden copy, but the actual weapon that had been owned by Edward Estur. It was made from an early form of tempered steel, and in its hilt, a twinkling yellow-green chrysoberyl gemstone was mounted. The graven effigy of the knight is dressed in chain mail, with a shield upon its left arm. The figure has its legs crossed, signifying that the knight fought in the crusades. The wooden effigy is said to be a representation of Edward Estur, a knight who returned from the crusade of 1365 with a serious head wound that left him an amnesiac.

Lucy Lightfoot developed a strange fixation for the carving of Edward Estur. The teenager would stand and stare at the effigy of the knight for hours. She even joined the congregation of St Olave's and became a regular worshipper there. One sunny afternoon at St Olave's, she stood in silence, bathed in the rainbow of light pouring from the stained-glass windows of the church, lost in blissful contemplation of Edward Estur, when the rector of the church approached the chancel and startled her with a query.

"Why do you stand so, Lucy?" he asked the girl.

Lucy awoke from her daydream and seemed unable to answer him. She blushed, looked at her hands, then told the rector: "I love to be with him. I long to accompany him on his adventures, if only in my thoughts and dreams."

The rector advised Lucy to go out into the sun, where she would meet real friends and companions, instead of being infatuated with a knight who had been dead for over four centuries.

"He's long turned to dust, Lucy. You are seeking the living among the dead," he remarked with a sympathetic smile.

Lucy was infuriated by his dismissive remark, and shook her head sternly.

"No! Edward isn't dead,"

She seemed as if she was about to burst into tears, and hurried out of the church.

On the morning of 13 June 1831, at around half-past ten, Lucy Lightfoot rode to St Olave's and left her horse tethered at the church gate. She entered the building – and was never seen again. That morning, a strange darkness blotted out the morning sun. The birds ceased their singing in the trees, and dogs bayed at the lowering sky. The eerie light was reminiscent of a solar eclipse, but records show that no such occultation of the sun took place on that date. A most violent thunderstorm exploded over the darkened skies, and dazzling forks of lightning were seen to strike St Olave's Church. A heavy rain fell on the area and continued for hours. Crops were destroyed by the bizarre, unseasonal weather, and many fields and roads became flooded.

The ominous shadow across the land lifted in the afternoon, and Farmer George Brewster, who was a good friend of Edward Lightfoot, left the shelter of a merchant's house and rode home. On the way, he noticed Lucy's frantic-looking horse, still tethered to the gate of St Olave's churchyard. He went into the church and found it empty. The rector was informed of Lucy's strange vanishing act, and he visited the chancel of the church, where he noticed something odd. The misericord that the wooden knight had held had been wrenched from its position and now lay in pieces on the floor. Furthermore, the jewel that had been set into the hilt was missing.

Edward Lightfoot offered a huge reward to anyone who could find his beloved daughter, but the money went unclaimed. Fields were searched and lakes were dragged. A well was even explored, but Lucy Lightfoot could not be found – except within the pages of a book, and this is where the story takes an intriguing twist. Thirty-five years after Lucy Lightfoot's disappearance, a Methodist minister in the Scilly Isles, the Reverend Samuel Trelawney, was researching the history of the last crusades, when he came across an old, yellowing manuscript, written by a crusader.

The manuscript's author was Phillipe de Mezieres, a crusader who had served Peter I of Cyprus as his Chancellor. Mezieres had been the logistical expert responsible for organising the crusade of 1365 which had resulted in the sack of Alexandria. The Reverend Trelawney traced his finger along the old French words on the parchment, then lit an extra candle, because he thought his eyes were playing tricks on him. But he was not mistaken at all. The name 'Lucy Lightfoot' was mentioned in the manuscript. Trelawney scratched his bald pate and wondered why that name was so familiar. Then he recalled the mysterious disappearance of Lucy Lightfoot 35 years before on the Isle of Wight. The Reverend adjusted his pince-nez glasses and continued to read the narrative of Phillipe de Mezieres. Whilst in London in November 1363, the King of Cyprus had asked for volunteers to help his crusade. Several knights offered the king their services – including one Edward Estur.

This particular knight entered the service of the King of Cyprus, and Edward brought a beautiful maiden from the Isle of Wight, named Lucy Lightfoot, with him. Edward and Lucy journeyed to Cyprus, and he left her on the island in the autumn of 1365 to embark on the crusade. Edward sailed with his fellow crusaders to Alexandria, which fell to their military might on 10 October. Edward and the other soldiers then embarked on another expedition to pillage the coast of Syria. Unfortunately, Edward Estur sustained a serious head injury when the curved blade of a heavy Saracen sword glanced off his skull, rendering him unconscious. For four months, Edward's condition remained critical. Expecting him to die, his comrades put him on a ship at Alexandria that took him home to England. Edward later made a startling recovery, but found himself unable to remember anything about his past. People mentioned Lucy Lightfoot to him, the maiden he loved and had sworn to marry one day, but Edward's amnesia had blotted out all memories of his beau. Meanwhile, Lucy waited three long and painful years for her lover to return from the crusade, and eventually left for Corsica, where she is said to have married a fisherman.

Upon his deathbed, Edward began to cry, and was said to have uttered Lucy's name before drawing his last breath. In the last seconds of his life he evidently had remembered the girl he had once idolised. The knight was buried in Gatcombe on the Isle of Wight, and a tomb was subsequently raised over his grave, crowned by an oaken effigy of the knight. A short bejewelled sword was placed in the hand of the effigy to symbolise the Order of the Sword awarded to Edward by the King of Cyprus.

What exactly took place at St Olave's on that June morning may never be known. Was Lucy Lightfoot transported back to the fourteenth century by some timeslip that might have been caused by the furious electrical storm? The Church frowns on such stories, and has tried for many years to dispel and debunk the Lightfoot tale. One priest who once publicly denounced the tale as a mere legend, later admitted that the Church authorities had instructed him to denounce the incident. He later retired from the priesthood, after admitting that he believed that Lucy had somehow travelled back to the time of the crusades. The priest was heavily criticised for his views, but retaliated by remarking that the Bible – which was once sworn upon in a court of law – contains accounts of Jonah living in the belly of a whale, as well as other stories which could be construed as being just as far-fetched as the strange tale of Lucy Lightfoot.


## Seeing Double

Ray Brunner of Irby Heath related the following strange story to me when I attended the Wirral Show in 2001. In 1969, when Ray was 32, he worked at the offices of an electrical contractor in Birkenhead. One blisteringly hot summer's day, the window in the office of Mr Meake, the firm's boss, became stuck, so he summoned one of his staff from downstairs to try and open it. One of the workforce came up and started to tackle the window, and moments later, another member of staff knocked at the boss's door.

"Come in," said Mr Meakes, without lifting his head from a letter he was reading.

A small bespectacled man named Graham Corbett entered.

"Yes, Corbett, what is it?"

"It's about Brunner, sir."

Meakes still hadn't raised his face to look at the diminutive employee.

"Yes, what about him?'

"Well, I see you have given him another day off, sir … " Corbett began.

"Huh?" Meakes looked up at last with a puzzled expression.

"Well, sir, he probably telephoned you to say he was sick but he's actually in a betting shop. I just passed the bookmakers round the corner while I was on my lunch break and saw him go in there."

"Well you should get your glasses changed, Corbett, because Mr Brunner has been here for the last 15 minutes, fixing the window." Mr Meakes told him, and he nodded round the corner of the L-shaped room, to the spot where Brunner was busy oiling the hinges of the troublesome window.

"Oh, that's strange," Corbett muttered, after turning to see his workmate standing at the window with an incensed look on his face.

"Beat it , Corbett, and get your eyes tested," said Mr Meakes, and he watched the small red-faced man nodding and walking towards the door.

It later transpired that Ray Brunner had some sort of twin he knew nothing of, because many more people, including his girlfriend, brother and best friend also saw Ray's double in various places, always at times when Ray was actually still at work. In one instance, Ray's brother was on the ferris wheel at the fair in New Brighton, when he was shocked to see Ray's replica walking about below. At the time, the real Ray was busy at work in Birkenhead. His double was then seen days later by Ray's mother as she shopped on a busy Birkenhead Street. She shouted at the person who she thought was her son, but the man did not even react; he simply walked on. What made the matter more sinister was the fact that the look-alike was wearing the same clothes Ray that had been wearing on the day, and this was always the case with each sighting.

Ray Brunner's twin was possibly a phantasm of himself, otherwise known in the world of the occult as a 'doppelganger' – a German word meaning 'double walker'. A doppelganger is also known as a 'fetch' in Celtic folklore, and a 'wraith' in English occult lore.

Doppelgangers are ghostly doubles of a living person, often someone who is perhaps seriously ill, or experiencing an emotional crisis. The appearance of a doppelganger is often said to be a sign portending the death of its flesh and blood counterpart, but this is just a legend, possibly based upon the story of the poet Shelley encountering his doppelganger shortly before he was drowned. Ray Brunner was certainly unsettled by the regular identical vision of him that was seen by so many.

# Creepy Coincidences

## Saved from Certain Death

In 1877, a carpenter, his wife and his mother, considered moving into an old farmhouse on the outskirts of Thingwall. The carpenter was Jem Tobin, aged 41 and his wife, who at 19, was less than half his age, was Joan.

Jem Tobin's mother started to act very strangely when her son decided to buy the farmhouse. Old Mrs Tobin was dubious, saying the place had a reputation for being haunted, and she had pleaded with him to buy another property instead.

Nevertheless, Jem and his wife moved into the house and he set up one of the six rooms as his workshop. Within days, he was toiling away making furniture and other items to support his wife and mother. It was his plan to hire an apprentice when he'd made sufficient money from his carpentry.

One day, Jem was on his cart, taking some furniture he'd made to a local farmer's house, when he came upon an alarming sight. He spotted Joan standing near the local well, and a young man was holding her in his arms. The couple were looking into one another's eyes, and they both seemed so entranced by one another, that neither of them noticed Jem's cart in the distance.

Jem was devastated, and when he delivered the furniture to the farmer, he was hardly able to speak. The farmer noticed his subdued manner and asked him if he was feeling unwell. Jem shook his head, took the money, and quietly returned home, feeling incredibly depressed. He had always feared the age difference between himself and his wife, although Joan had always reassured him that he was the only man she could ever love.

Later on, when Joan returned from an errand, she seemed to be lost in deep thought about something; she didn't seem herself. Suddenly, she asked Jem a strange question.

"Jem …" she began quietly, "if someone loved you, and you didn't feel the same way about them, would you tell them, and break their heart, or stay just away from them?"

Jem felt a lump in his throat. He knew she was talking about him.

"I would tell him," he sighed. "Why do you ask, Joan?"

Joan seemed awkward as she replied, "Oh, I just wondered. Just a foolish thought I had."

For the rest of that week, Joan seemed very distant, and kept staring into space, lost in intense thought about something – or someone.

Jem also fell into deep reverie. He convinced himself that Joan had fallen out of love with him and had fallen in love with the young man he'd seen embracing her by the well. Unable to bear the idea, he decided to end it all; as far as he was concerned life would be unbearable without her. Jem Tobin set to work building a contraption that would make his suicide easy. It was a six-foot long beam of timber with a sharp axe-head fixed to the top. The bottom of the wooden beam was hinged, and fixed to a wooden base. A small length of rope was tied around the top of the beam near the axe-head, and the other end was tethered to the wall. Jem then fixed a candle-stick to the piece of wood, and put a short candle in it.

Once this candle was lit, it would take a few minutes to burn down to a point where it would burn through part of the rope. The beam would then be released, and it would lean sideways and fall. The axehead would completely sever Jem Tobin's head, which would already be resting on a pillow on a wooden chopping block. Jem had considered everything. To calm himself down, he would drink as much whisky as possible, then he'd light the candle, and lie down to await his doom.

Jem began putting his plan into practise on a hot summer morning while his mother and Joan were in town buying groceries. He left a heartfelt suicide note to Joan, saying he loved her so much that he could never bear to live without her. He then went into his workshop and bolted the door. He swigged down half the bottle of whisky, and tried to light the candle with his trembling hands. On the third attempt, he managed to light the wick. He then took up his position on the floor. He lay down and rested his head on the pillow, and gulped down more whiskey. Those few minutes were the longest in his life. He watched as the rope slowly started to smoulder. He looked at the sharpened axe head and the heavy wooden beam that would soon lean forward and fall heavily. Then he'd be decapitated instantly. He hoped it would be swift. The smouldering rope twanged, and the beam shuddered. Upon seeing this, Jem fainted. The rope was still smouldering. It wouldn't take long now.

Jem Tobin awoke to see a blue sky with a single cloud floating by. He thought he was in paradise. Then he focused on two vague outlines before him and noticed that Joan and his mother were leaning over him. They had returned from the village, and after finding the suicide note, Joan had smashed a window to get into the workshop. She and his mother had dragged him outside.

She kissed Jem, whispering that the man who had hugged her at the well was just an admirer, and that she didn't like him, although he had claimed that he loved Joan. That was why Joan had asked Jem the peculiar question a few days earlier, she had been talking about her unwanted admirer. Joan was overwhelmed with emotion as she told Jem that no one on earth could take his place.

Although the words were everything he needed to hear, Jem was distracted by a niggling thought; he was baffled as to why the candle had not burned through the rope, because they said they had found him unconscious almost 40 minutes after he had lit the wick. Something must have somehow blown that candle out.

Jem's mother felt certain that it had been the ghost of Jem's father, because, she revealed, he had committed suicide in that exact cottage just after Jem had been born. He had fallen into depression after the failure of his crops, and found himself heavily in debt. He had hanged himself. It seemed Mrs Tobin's dislike of the farmhouse had been more than justified.

That night, Jem and his wife embraced one another tightly in bed. A candle burned on the bedside table. Jem whispered goodnight to his wife, and she kissed him before turning over ready to fall asleep.

"Goodnight, father, wherever you are," Jem said in a low voice.

And he was convinced that he felt the gentle touch of a hand pat his head. Then someone blew the candle out ...

## Strange Coincidences

I'm sure you, the reader, have experienced the eerie phenomenon of a strange coincidence. Most of us have been in the situation where we are thinking about a person we haven't seen for years, when suddenly, the telephone will ring and the person we've been thinking about is on the other end of the line. Mathematicians often explain coincidences away as mere chance events, but I am sure that they are more than that. Could coincidences be proof that some intelligent force is at work in the Cosmos?

In June 2002, I was talking about the nature of coincidences on the *Roger Lyons Show* on Radio Merseyside. I happened to say that the National Lotto numbers, which are picked by random number generating machines, are often anything but random. The numbers often come out in consecutive runs. A listener in Wallasey emailed me asking me to explain what I meant. I emailed him back, giving him an example of my theory. The example I gave off the top of my head was "forty-two, forty-three, forty-four" – and on the following Saturday, the man emailed me to say he had won ten pounds because he had chosen the three numbers which I had mentioned in my example, and they had been drawn by the random number generator MERLIN on the Lotto Show. The numbers drawn had been: 1, 20, 42, 43, 44, 49.

That same week, a man in Blackpool rang me at the radio station and said that he had applied my theory of 'sequential clusters' by choosing the numbers 5, 6, 7 on the Irish Lotto – and those numbers had come up. The strange groupings of Lotto results can be explained by what I call the 'cluster effect'. Every mathematician knows that a random distribution of events produces strange clusters. A mundane example would be mixing cherries in a cake. According to common sense, the cherries should be distributed more or less evenly in the cake, but a cross section through any fruitcake will prove otherwise. The cherries gather in clusters. The same thing happens in an abstract way when the mathematical value of PI ($\pi$) is calculated. PI is a transcendental number that begins as 3.141592653589 ... and it continues to infinity. Its value has been computed to millions of places, and along the way, very strange clusters of numbers appear which are difficult to explain.

Some of the greatest minds in history have tackled the mystery of coincidence. Dr Paul Kammerer published the first systematic analysis of coincidence in 1919 in a book called *The Law of Seriality*. Dr Kammerer, who was the Director of the Institute of Experimental Biology in Vienna, had kept a diary noting all the coincidences he had experienced from the age of 20. He noted that certain numbers and specific phrases and names kept recurring and cropping up throughout the years with regular mathematical incidence, almost to the point of being part of some unknown algebraic formula. Kammerer concluded that what we interpreted as coincidence was merely the tip of a cosmic iceberg of which we were ignorant. Many decades later, a brilliant Nobel Prize-winning physicist named Wolfgang Pauli meditated on the nature of coincidence and formulated his 'Exclusion Principle' – a complex concept that explained how electrons were distributed within the atom.

The Swiss psychologist-philosopher, Professor Carl Gustav Jung, collaborated with Pauli to write a treatise called *Synchronicity, an acausal connecting principle*. Jung and Pauli hinted in the ground-breaking treatise that a single mysterious force was at work in the universe that is trying to impose its order on the chaos of human life. Was this force a living entity? Was it proof of God? Jung and Pauli were not prepared to stick their necks out that far to answer these questions.

Here are some cases with local connections where the long arm of coincidence has been eerily at work.

~

One night, in April 1939, a Wirral captain was at the helm of his ship when he suddenly realised that it was the exact date – 27 years to the very day – when the *Titanic* had gone down in 1912. The captain glanced at his watch and saw that it was the very same hour that the ill-fated liner had slid beneath the waves, and if that wasn't coincidental enough, the captain also realised that his ship was moving through the very same area of the Atlantic where the *Titanic* had been scarred by an iceberg. The captain slowed the vessel down, and minutes later, a lookout shouted that there was an iceberg ahead. Moments later, a huge iceberg glided silently towards the ship and missed it by a matter of feet. The ship that had been involved in this near miss, on the anniversary of the *Titanic* disaster, was the *Titanian*.

~

Mrs Gloria Chattersby Phillips – who originally came from Bromborough – emigrated to the United States in the 1920s, and settled in Manhattan. In August 1921 a man named Servando Cazarli discovered that the beautiful Mrs Chattersby Phillips was having an affair, and threatened to tell her husband unless she paid him $1000 each week. Each week, on Wednesday evening, Cazarli would call, collect the money, then leave.

She found herself engulfed by growing debts, and one Tuesday night, Mrs Chattersby Phillips could take no more, and decided to end her life. She opened the window of her fourth floor apartment in a calm and determined frame of mind. Glancing down at the lights below, she took a deep breath, closed her eyes and jumped out.

By sheer chance, she landed on a man who was on the walkway below and he was killed instantly. Gloria suffered nothing more a than a dislocated shoulder. Reconciled to her survival, the coincidence which really shook her to the bone, was that the man she had killed was none other than Servando Cazarli. It seemed that he'd decided to call a day earlier than usual for his $1000.

At the time, Mrs Gloria Chattersby claimed to have tripped and fallen out of the window, insisting that the awful occurrence had been an accident. It wasn't until many years later that she told the police what had really happened. Apparently they had said the incident had been a case of poetic justice.

~

On 5 December 1664, a ship with 81 passengers sank in the Menai Strait off North Wales. There was one survivor: a red-haired man named Hugh Williams. On 5 December 1785, another ship sank in the Menai Strait, and of the 80 passengers, only one person survived: another red-haired man named Hugh Williams. Stranger still, on 5 December 1800, yet another ship sank in the Menai Strait with 25 people on board, and all the passengers drowned – all except for yet another red-headed man – his name was Hugh Williams.

~

The *Liverpool Echo* of 21 July 1975 reported that two brothers from Liverpool went to Bermuda on two separate occasions. Both were killed on their holidays, but as if that wasn't awful enough, they were both killed by the same man, a taxi driver. Stranger still, the taxi driver was carrying the same passenger each time; the brothers had both been riding the same model moped; the crashes had both occurred on the same stretch of street – in the exact same spot. What makes this set of cruel coincidences even more chilling, is the fact that the brothers died exactly one year apart on the exact same date.

~

In the summer of 1997, Tammy, a student from New Brighton, journeyed across the Mersey to visit her aunt in Wavertree. Finding that her aunt was not at home, Tammy decided to wait in a nearby public house called the Wellington, hoping she would return home soon. As Tammy entered the pub, a man named Jimmy noticed her and was struck by her beauty. Moments later, the Beatles' song *I Will* started playing on the jukebox, adding an air of romance to the moment.

Jimmy offered to buy Tammy a drink, and it wasn't long before they were chatting away together. Jimmy begged her for her mobile number, and she finally gave it to him. Jimmy and Tammy ended up dating and by August 1998 the relationship had become serious enough to drive Jimmy to the jewellery shop of Ernest Jones to purchase an engagement ring. Jimmy and Tammy rendezvoused at the Wellington pub days later. At an opportune moment, Jimmy got down on his bended knee and took the small velvet-lined box containing the ring from his inside jacket pocket. Tammy seemed to be in shock. Jimmy opened the tiny lid of the box, and Tammy looked at the dazzling diamond ring with tears in her eye.

"Tammy, will you please marry me, girl?" Jimmy asked, totally oblivious to the bemused drinkers looking over.

"I will," Tammy replied, in a choked voice.

At that moment, a song selected by a man who had never been seen in that pub before suddenly played on the jukebox. That song was *I Will* – the same Lennon and McCartney love song that had played that summer afternoon in the pub when Jimmy had first set eyes upon Tammy.

The happy couple married in July 2001, but that was not where the coincidences ended. In 2002, Tammy gave birth to a baby girl. Being a big softie at heart, Jimmy wept with joy when he first held his baby daughter. By now, the couple were living in Moreton and Jimmy drove his wife and new little daughter home. They sat on the sofa cuddling the baby, when Jimmy noticed that the radio he had left on was playing 'their song', *I Will*.

~

A series of coincidences of a much darker nature were related to me by a retired policeman, Alan Smith, who now lives in Willaston. In the 1970s, Smith had served as a constable in Erdington, a village lying five miles outside Birmingham. In 1975, PC Smith had been involved in a murder investigation. The date was 27 May. A 20-year-old nurse named Barbara Forrest had been raped, then strangled at a flooded sandpit in Erdington. Her body was found in long grass.

PC Smith's friend, Tony Deane, was a police archivist, and one day, the two men were having lunch in the police canteen when Deane said he had come across an amazing series of coincidences that seemed to link the Barbara Forrest murder with a nineteenth century murder. After lunch, Smith accompanied Deane to the police archives, where he showed him a dusty bundle of papers.

"Listen to this," Deane said, as he studied the old handwriting of the files. "On 27 May 1817, the body of 20-year old Mary Ashford was found in a flooded sandpit in Erdington. Like Barbara Forrest, she was not only the same age, she shared the same birthday. Like Miss Forrest, Miss Ashford was also raped and then strangled, and according to this map, she was found in the exact same spot as Miss Forrest, only 157 years before – to the exact same day."

"Coincidence," was PC Smith's monotone reply, but his friend continued to reel off even more eerie parallels between the two murder cases.

"Both of these girls, Ashford and Forrest, had visited their best friends on the evening of Whit Monday to change into a new dress before going to the local dance party. Now, here's another weird thing; Barbara Forrest's friends said that just before she was killed, the girl made strange prophetic remarks about her impending fate. Barbara Forrest allegedly said: 'This is going to be my unlucky week. I just know it. Don't ask me why.'"

"What are you getting at?" PC Smith asked, beginning to feel uneasy.

The archivist told him: "It says here that Mary Ashford said: 'I have bad feelings about the week to come and I know not why.'"

PC Smith considered the astounding coincidences.

"Okay, let's say this is a case of history, or murder – repeating itself, I wonder if the killers' names will be the same on both occasions?"

"That's a good point," the police archivist said, and scanned the end of the old yellowed page he had been reading. "The man they arrested for the murder of Mary Ashford was one Abraham Thornton, but the case against him fell apart, and he was acquitted."

"So we should be looking for someone with that name?" PC Smith replied.

"But supernatural mumbo jumbo isn't enough. We'd need more than that, mate."

The two men left the archives, and when they went upstairs, they passed a man being brought into the station. He was being charged with the murder of Barbara Forrest. Inconceivably, the murder suspect's surname was indeed Thornton. PC Smith and the archivist were completely stunned by this astronomical coincidence which had crowned all the other uncanny coincidences which connected two murders committed 157 years apart.

Stranger still, like the Thornton of 1817, the Thornton of 1975 was also subsequently released after being acquitted of the murder of Barbara Forrest.


# A Friend in Need

In May 1971, John, a 38-year-old black man from Toxteth, started seeing spots before his eyes. Naturally disconcerted, he reassured himself by assuming that it was high blood pressure, but then his eyesight also became blurred. He assumed it was his age, and that he'd be wearing glasses soon. However, a few days later, he woke up, and attempted to yawn, but found he was unable to open his mouth. He thought he had lockjaw, so he quickly dressed and rushed to the doctor's surgery on Chatham Street, where he barged in, waving a note on which he had written about his alarming condition, and was soon taken to the Royal Hospital.

After several extensive tests on John, his head was X-rayed and a decision was made to operate on his brain, as the doctors had pinpointed a blood-clot there. John made a full recovery, but when he came home to his house on Windsor Street, he felt as if he was a changed man. Before the operation, he had, by his own admission, been a lazy speaker, with a low, disinterested voice, but now he spoke clearly, and seemed altogether more extrovert. There was also another change taking place in John that baffled him and those around him.

One afternoon, a dog was knocked down on Admiral Street. The animal's rear legs seemed to be broken and the owners did not hold out a lot of hope about the its survival. John saw the crowd gathered around the injured dog and he walked over to see what had happened. He knelt down by the injured creature, and felt a strange urge to put his hands over its head. As he did so, people looked on, bemused. Suddenly, the animal yelped, and the dog's owner swore at John and asked him what he had done. In that moment, the dog leapt to its feet. Its tail wagged, and then it walked away, admittedly a little unsteadily at first, before running into the butcher's shop, where the butcher regularly offered the dog a bone.

News of that strange incident spread around the district of Granby and the rest of the neighbourhood, and John was soon being asked to heal people. Not once did he take anything in return. His miraculous abilities turned him towards religion and he started to study the Rastafarian teachings.

It was after he had moved to London that something amazing took place which made headline news. John was travelling on the underground, on his way to see a Rastafarian friend, when he started to see visions. The subject of these visions was a well-to-do man who was looking at blueprints and plans of buildings. John sensed that he was an architect, and that he was deeply upset and depressed by something. John wondered why he was getting these insights into another man's troubles, when suddenly, he had another vision. This time he could see the architect jumping from a railway platform on the London Underground on to the line. John felt that the man had actually jumped at that very moment, and he somehow knew that the train he was now travelling in would soon run over the architect and slice him in two. The Toxteth man jumped to his feet, startling the commuters in the compartment. He pulled the emergency handle with all his might. The train wheels squealed as the brakes automatically came on and sparks lit up the tunnel. People were thrown all over the carriage as the train ground to a noisy halt.

A huge man with a skinhead haircut began to scream racist profanities at John for stopping the train and threatened to give him a beating.

"Brother, I had to do it, there's a man on the line," was all that John could offer by means of reply.

The transport police and other officials soon arrived and saw all the fingers pointing at John. He was arrested. They shoved him on to the platform and led him up the steps on to the streets of London. But then came the strange news from below.

A London Transport official approached John, who stood quietly and did not struggle.

"Okay, sir. What's your game?" he asked John.

John was puzzled.

"What are you talking about?"

The official explained to the policemen holding John, "There was a man lying on the tracks. He's out of his mind, but all this must have been set up for some reason."

John grew uncomfortable. He didn't know what was going on. He was immediately taken to a police station, but after a long interview, he was released. They dismissed his talk of visions as the likely result of smoking too much 'ganja'.

On the following day, John's friend, Brother Keith, showed him the newspapers. On the front of the *Evening Standard* and the *Guardian*, and inside the staid pages of *The Times*, there was a very interesting story. The articles said that a young architect had suffered a nervous breakdown and had thrown himself into the path of an oncoming train on the London Underground. People had turned away in horror, expecting him to be killed, but the tube train had suddenly stopped, just in time, and the man was saved. The papers claimed that a certain unbalanced Liverpool man had unwittingly saved the suicidal architect by recklessly pulling the communication cord. The strange incident was explained away in all the newspapers as a coincidence, but only John knew the truth.

The mystery deepened when the man John had saved caught up with him months later. The man, named Dennis, tracked him down to a bookshop where the latter worked in Highbury. The two men were speechless for a moment. John gradually recognised the architect and vice versa. The two men had, in fact, been close childhood friends with an amazing bond that seemed to transcend reality. In 1945, John and Dennis had played together as 12-year-olds in Birkenhead. At the time, John had been staying with his Aunt Pauline after his parents in Liverpool had split up. The next door neighbour's son – Dennis – had been John's best friend. Dennis was a weak, sickly boy who suffered from extreme short-sightedness. He was always getting into scrapes, and without fail, John was always the one who came to his rescue. One day John was walking down Ashville Road by Birkenhead Park when he saw two ruffians stealing Dennis's cricket bat and ball. John intervened and made the yobs hand the items back to his friend. On another occasion, whilst holidaying in Southport, Dennis found himself sinking into the sands as the tide was coming in. Somehow, John had managed to free him. Now, 26 years on, his old friend had once again saved his life.

John had a long chat with Dennis, who told him that he had attempted suicide because his wife had filed for divorce. It just so happened that John needed new lodgings, so he moved in to Dennis's home, where, gradually, he instilled enough confidence into his old friend to enable him to go on in life. Sixteen months later, Dennis met a beautiful secretary, and ended up marrying her. Today, the two men remain great friends, and the amazing, strangely predictive bond between them is as strong as ever.

# Flickers of the Future

I am always fascinated by dreams of the future. The readers of my books and column in the *Merseymart,* and the listeners to my radio broadcasts have contacted me many times to report strange premonitions they have experienced whilst asleep.

In late March 1999, a Mrs Creane of Eastham wrote to me about a series of nightmares she had been having for the past couple of weeks. The subject of the bad dreams was a plane falling out of the sky on to a housing estate. During the nightmares, Mrs Creane was looking up into the blue sky, paralysed with fear as she watched a passenger jet falling in slow motion out of the sky. She could hear people screaming and cars smashing into one another as their drivers tried desperately to get out of the way of the falling jet. Mrs Creane could feel her heart pounding as the jet turned and twisted as it nose-dived – and at the last moment before it fell on her, she was always able to close her eyes, but she would feel the ground shake and could hear screams that came to an abrupt end as the jet exploded.

She would then usually find herself screaming out loud and sit bolt upright in bed, her body moist with sweat. Mr Creane became very concerned about the recurring nightmares his wife was experiencing and advised her to see a doctor. Instead, she wrote to me, as she believed that the nightmares were premonitions of a real future event that was going to happen.

I visited Mrs Creane, and over a cup of tea, I asked her to describe the type of plane to me. She said it had three engines. I was a bit dubious about this, until she explained that the third engine was situated at the back of the plane. Just beneath the vertical tail fin. The other two engines were located under each wing. The only other thing she could recall was that a thin blue stripe ran along the fuselage from the nose. Armed with these details, I visited a friend named Callum who is a plane fanatic, and he told me that the plane the woman was describing was a Lockheed Tristar jet. Callum is not a believer in the world of the supernatural, but he was interested in the woman's dream. He said he would try and find out if any Tristars were due to fly to, or from, the local airports.

Weeks later I received an email from Callum. He had scanned an article from the *Knutsford Guardian,* dated 14 April 1999. The piece was about a defective Lockheed Tristar that had flown over Merseyside and Cheshire at an altitude less than eight-hundred feet. The Peruvian-owned Tristar struggled to climb over Knutsford. The crew had been paid £25,000 each to man the flight to America via Iceland. A fortnight earlier, the jet – which had been parked outside at the airport for more than two years – had been forced back to Manchester when its navigational instruments failed. The two engines – one beneath the tail fin and the other beneath the left wing – were the only ones that were working. An empty engine housing was carried on the other wing.

Was this dangerously neglected jet the plane Mrs Creane had seen falling out of the sky in her recurring nightmares? I hope that it was just an eerie coincidence, but cannot rule out the possibility that perhaps the Eastham woman foresaw a horrifying plane crash, years or months into the future, perhaps somewhere over this region of the North West. I sincerely hope it was nothing more than a bad dream. Mrs Creane, incidentally, has not had the terrifying dream since May 1999.

Not all dreams of the future are harbingers of doom. One peculiar dream ended in the dreamer being married. In October 2000, Margot, a 44-year-old Bebington housewife, had a series of strange dreams about a place she had never visited in her life. The setting of the dreams was always a sunny beach, populated by tanned people, some carrying surfboards. The sunny weather, golden sands and clear blue water reminded Margot of the coastal waters of California which she had seen on television shows like *Baywatch*. In Margot's recurring dream, she could see a man with curly light brown hair, sitting in a deckchair, scribbling in a notepad. He wore a pale lilac tee shirt and white shorts. In the dreams, Margot never saw his face. The persistent dream did not make sense to her.

Margot was a widow. Her husband had died two years before, and her 15-year-old son David still missed him as much as she did. Margot had recently bought her only child a personal computer, and already, David was hooked on the Internet and PC games, whereas Margot was clueless where computers were concerned. She didn't even really know how to click a mouse properly.

On the night of 22 October 2000, at around half-past ten, Margot dozed off in an armchair as she was completing the crossword in a Sunday newspaper. She had the same recurring dream about the stranger at the beach, but this time she saw a series of letters and symbols in front of her eyes. They were black, and printed on a white background. The first four letters spelt the word 'Mike'. Margot suddenly realised she was dreaming, and just before she woke up, she had a good look at the strange message. It read: 'mikezzz@ex'

As soon as she was fully awake, Margot used the pen with which she had been completing the crossword, to quickly jot down the peculiar message. She then reflected on the dream for a few moments before making herself a cup of tea. Shortly afterwards, her son David left his bedroom and came downstairs after an intensive two-hour session of surfing the Net on his computer. He grabbed the newspaper to check the TV listings, when he saw the partial email address his mother had written down in the margin of the crossword page. He asked her whose email address it was.

"I don't know, I saw it in a dream," she explained, feeling a bit embarrassed. "I think, though I'm not sure, that it ended in 'com' or something," she added.

David was intrigued. "It might be Mike triple Z, at excite dot com," her son suggested, excitedly.

All this was over Margot's head. His mother glanced over his shoulder at the word she'd written.

"Is that what that is? An email address thingy?" she asked curiously.

David nodded, and he stood up and announced: "Mum, I'll send an email to this address and tell the person you saw it in a dream!"

"No, don't. They'll think I'm nuts; just leave it."

But David was already on his way back to his bedroom.

"David! Don't overrule me, son. I've just told you you're not to do that!" Margot shouted up the stairs after him.

"Chill out, Mum!" came the reply.

David sent an email to the address mikezzz@excite.com, explaining how his mother had seen the address in a dream. When he came back downstairs, Margot chided her son.

"I hope you haven't told them where we live; haven't you heard of all these stalkers on the Net?" she told David, waving her finger in his face.

The next day, David checked his email inbox and saw that mikezzz@excite.com had replied. His name was Mike Falkner. He was an oneirologist – or dream researcher – working in Los Angeles. David surmised that the three z's in the email address probably symbolised sleep, as those letters were traditionally used by cartoonists to depict a sleeping person.

Mike Falkner was naturally fascinated by David's claim, and told the boy to email his telephone number. David did this, even though he knew it was unwise to do so. That night the telephone rang in Margot's home and she answered it. She was surprised to hear an American accent. Mike Falkner introduced himself, and asked her to relate the dream in which she had seen his email address. When Margot described the man with curly brown hair at the beach, scribbling in a notebook, there was a long pause at the other end of the line.

"You just described me, I think," Mike gasped.

Margot described the clothes the man in the dream wore: the white shorts and pale lilac tee shirt – and Mike said he had worn those exact items last week. Furthermore, he often relaxed at the beach and either wrote down notes and ideas in a notebook, or used his laptop computer.

An email correspondence between the Bebington housewife and the Californian oneirologist started which lasted for three months, and soon Mike flew to England to meet up with Margot. In the summer of 2001, Margot and David went to stay with Mike for a few weeks in Los Angeles, and at the time of writing, Mike and Margot are engaged to marry – all because of a dream.

# Hauntings

## Chilling Chimes

In February 2002, Barbara from Birkenhead went to a car boot sale in Chester with her boyfriend Liam. They went to the car boot sale so early, that it was still dark when they pulled into the carpark, so Liam had to fetch a flashlight from the boot.

Barbara found and bought a few items. One item in particular that took her fancy was a small, black, shiny musical box with an intricate gold heart pattern inlaid on the lid. She had been charmed by the delicate detail on it, and was pleased with herself for buying it, for only £3. She opened it, and it played the main theme to the opera *The Merry Widow*.

When the couple arrived back home later that day, Liam suddenly called for her attention.

"What's that?" he asked, looking around.

"What's what?" Barbara replied, without paying much attention, until she heard it too.

It was clearly the chimes of *The Merry Widow*, but Barbara could not understand why they could hear the tune, as the unusual little box wasn't in the room, it was definitely upstairs in the bedroom where she had placed it. Barbara went upstairs to check. She found the box on her dressing table where she had proudly positioned it minutes earlier, and picked it up. Opening it, she heard the chimes begin. She snapped closed the lid, silencing the music, and placed it back on the dresser.

When Barbara went to work on the following day, she could not get the haunting song out of her mind, and stranger still, neither could her boyfriend. Liam worked in a garage, and he first noticed the spectral melody as the boss was talking to him in the office. The chimes in his head became such a distraction, that Liam couldn't concentrate on his work. All he could hear was the accursed tune, and it tormented him to distraction, so much so, that he had to go home. As he drove home, he was so affected, that he wondered if someone in the garage had somehow spiked his tea with some hallucinogenic drug.

When he got home, he was surprised to find that Barbara was already there. It transpired that she too had come home from work because of the haunting chimes relentlessly replaying in her mind. They had driven her to absolute distraction as well. Later that day, she showed a neighbour the box, who commented that the music was strangely catchy. Then, that evening, the neighbour reported that the eerie tune had invaded her mind as well. It was even affecting her sleep, because she could hear the irritating notes playing over and over again in her dreams.

A call was made to me at the studios of Radio Merseyside, and I visited Barbara and Liam's home in Birkenhead to take a look at the mysterious musical box. Wary of its reputation, I was not too keen to open it, even though my curiosity urged me to do so. Barbara, Liam and their neighbour nervously suggested that I should open the box elsewhere.

As I examined it, I could find no markings on the outside which might have provided the name of its manufacturer. Undaunted, I later visited the car boot sale where Barbara had purchased the box, and even managed to trace the man who had sold it to her, but all he could remember was that an old woman had given him the box for nothing at a car boot sale in Rock Ferry.

I decided to mention the musical box on the radio, and described the tune it played. Immediately, a number of listeners called the station. Some claimed that they, too, had been afflicted with the never-ending tune after listening to the box. One woman who visited a hearing specialist was diagnosed with tinnitus, but believed her condition had something to do with the mysterious black musical box and its ceaseless melody.

Then came the breakthrough.

A caller named Mr Lewis telephoned me and accurately described the intricate heart-shaped pattern on the lid. He said that, after he had opened that exact same box in 1975, he had been unable to get the tune out of his head. It became so bad, that he had to sleep with the radio playing on his bedside table to drown out the tune. In 1977, the tune had finally faded away, but it had been such an intrusion into his life, that it had broken up his marriage. I asked him how he had come into possession of the musical box, and Mr Lewis said that he had moved into a house in Rock Ferry in 1974 and had found it there, along with other items, including an old Welsh Bible. Mr Lewis had subsequently heard a strange tale from his new neighbours. They told him that the previous inhabitant of the house had poisoned himself many years ago in the 1920s. Beside his body, the man's wife had found the musical box lying open with the haunting melody still playing. It had undoubtedly been that same musical box with the gold heart on.

This is one story with no satisfactory ending. In this era, when radio stations and television programmes repeatedly bombard us with mindless pop tunes, it's easy to find yourself humming or whistling a catchy melody, but how can an old musical box implant such a devilishly interminable tune into the minds of those who innocently open its lid? And what is the significance of *The Merry Widow*? I remain baffled.


## The Amorous Ghost

In March 2002, Rosemary, a 55-year-old Bromborough woman, wrote to me at Radio Merseyside to offer her services as a medium. On air during the *Billy Butler Show*, I had mentioned the fact that many so-called psychics and mediums I had tested had been of little use to me during my investigations into the paranormal, as they had rarely even been able to supply me with the surname of a ghost or spirit that was haunting a house. In response to this remark, Rosemary wrote to me, asking if she could demonstrate her psychical talents. She told me that she could see and hear many spirits, and could occasionally 'read' the emotional impressions that had been absorbed by a variety of inanimate objects. This latter ability is known as psychometry, whereby the reader picks up the emotions, visual impressions and other data from the owner of an object such as a wedding ring, or cigarette case, for example.

One Spring day, about a week after receiving the letter, I visited Rosemary at her home, and was immediately struck by her beauty. She looked remarkably young for her age, and I assumed that the woman answering the door was her daughter. We chatted over tea and biscuits, and I asked her about her alleged abilities. Rosemary told me that from as far back as early childhood she had experienced supernatural goings on. As a child she had associated with a group of ghostly children in the back garden of her home in Birkenhead. One playmate had been an Edwardian teenager, while another member of the gang was from the 1930s, and wore a flat cap. Mary, a little blonde girl of about six years of age, who had died from a broken neck after falling out of a tree in 1869, had apparently been Rosemary's best friend. When the family relocated to Bebington, Rosemary had left in tears, watching from the back of the removal van as the ghostly companions stood huddled outside the house waving to her.

After the tea and biscuits, I decided to test Rosemary's psychometry faculty. I handed an object to her that was enclosed in a padded, manila envelope. I made it clear that she was not to open the envelope. Rosemary slowly moved her right palm over the envelope and then held it to her forehead.

"Oh! My God. Oh!" she gasped.

I waited, intrigued, for her to make further comments.

"I see blood. A woman dying. Two people."

Rosemary handed the envelope back to me and took deep breaths as she placed her hands on her head.

"What did you experience?" I asked her.

"A woman with dark hair, and a man hitting her with something. Piano keys. Her poor head. Oh my!" Rosemary grimaced as if she was suffering from a severe migraine.

The envelope contained a certain item loaned to me by a crime historian. A water colour painting by one Julia Wallace, who had been murdered in Liverpool in 1931. The killer, who was never identified, had battered Mrs Wallace over the head eleven times with an iron bar during his brutal attack, leaving the woman lying on the floor of her front parlour with her brains oozing out of the hole in her smashed skull. Near the body, was the piano that Mrs Wallace had often played – with its lid open. Rosemary's description of the murder scene – including the piano keys – was spot on.

A few other objects were also given to Rosemary to see if she could repeat her psychometry success. A box containing an unusual item puzzled the psychic. Rosemary talked of a vast darkness, of immense stretches of time, of infinity. At last came the description that convinced me.

"Stars. So bright, but they don't twinkle," Rosemary muttered as she held the box to her forehead.

"That's very good," I told her. "The box contains a small sample of a meteorite that fell in Wales in the nineteen-sixties."

I wondered how would Rosemary fare in a ghost investigation. After making a telephone call, I decided to take her to a haunting at a Victorian terraced house in Devonshire Park, where a top-hatted spectre had been seen in several houses in a street there.

An old widowed woman named Katie Wheeler greeted us at one of the allegedly haunted houses and escorted us into a back parlour, where her friend, 69-year-old Fred Goodwin, was waiting to welcome us.

The four of us sat at the table, and Katie related a very intriguing tale. In January she had met Fred at a bingo hall, and they had become good friends. They often went to the pub together, and also enjoyed walks around the Mersey and Victoria Parks. Fred interposed at this point and said that by early February, he had fallen in love with Katie, but being a rather bashful person, he found it difficult to express his feelings. He wanted her to give up her flat to come and live with him, but was scared of rejection, and couldn't bring himself to ask Katie to move in with him as his partner.

Fred decided he would write an old-fashioned love letter to Katie, telling her that he loved her and asking her to be his sweetheart. The letter was never posted. Fred put it in a drawer in his bedroom cabinet and decided he would tell Katie, face to face, just how he felt – eventually. When that would be was the thing though, because every time Fred tried to get the words out, he became tongue-tied. The one hope on the near horizon was Valentine's Day, 14 February. Fred bought a huge Valentine card and put the love letter in it. However, he watched the dates of the calendar each day as 14 February loomed nearer and nearer. On the eve of the most romantic date in the calendar, Fred decided he was being too forward. He should wait a little longer, he decided. However, when he searched the cabinet, he discovered that the Valentine card was missing. Fred searched his house from top to bottom, and could not find the card anywhere, and its disappearance truly baffled him.

On the following morning, shortly after eight o'clock, a single pink envelope landed on the doormat in the hall. Fred opened the envelope and saw it contained a Valentine card. His heart somersaulted. It was from Katie. 'I love you Fred,' Katie had written in the card.

Fred felt elated, yet also strongly regretted not having posted his Valentine and love letter to Katie.

"Faint heart never won a fair lady," he whispered to himself.

However, Katie called around later that day, and as soon as Fred opened the door, Katie looked at him in a way that said it all. The old woman's eyes were radiant with love for him. The couple gazed at each other, reading the unspoken mysterious language of love, and embraced and kissed like lovelorn teenagers. When they went inside Fred's house, Katie said that she would live with him, and she told Fred that the letter he'd put in the huge Valentine card had been the loveliest thing she'd ever read.

Fred was astounded. Someone or something had posted that letter – which did not even have a postage stamp – by hand to Katie's flat at precisely midnight, because Katie had heard her letterbox flap clang at that time. She'd been impressed by the fleet-footed Fred, because she had not heard him walk away down the street.

Fred later admitted to Katie that he had not posted the Valentine. She didn't believe him at first, but when he insisted, she wondered if there had been a supernatural explanation. The very night on which the Valentine arrived, Katie had detected the strange sweet aroma of violets. Later that same night, at around eleven-thirty, Katie had been cooking herself supper, when she turned around to see an oddly-dressed stranger standing in the far corner of the living room. It was the barely visible image of a young man, dressed in dark out-dated clothes. He wore a white, starched high collar and a tie. The youth's rosy-cheeked face was so friendly-looking, and he wore an innocent smile. Within a heartbeat, the apparition vanished. The ghostly intruder left Katie a little shaken.

Katie told Fred about the ghost, and expected him to think she was seeing things, but Fred believed in her and said he had never doubted the existence of spirits.

After hearing the remarkable account of the phantom postman, Rosemary said: "His name's Thomas. I think his full name is Thomas Pembroke."

Katie, Fred and I shot a startled look at Rosemary, who was gazing into the air as if she was lost in reverie.

"He lived in this house, Tom," she told me.

Katie clutched Fred's hand. She seemed a little unnerved by Rosemary's 'tuning-in' to the dearly departed amorous ghost.

"Upstairs in the attic, he says," Rosemary elaborated softly, then smiled and nodded to a space in front of the fireplace, indicating where the ghost was standing. "He's there, don't be scared."

Poor Katie turned her face to Fred's chest and closed her eyes as he hugged her.

"Oh, he's gone now. He's upstairs," Rosemary told me. "He's in the attic," she added.

"Why?" I asked the medium. "What's up there?"

"He wants to show you something," Rosemary said.

I asked Fred if it was possible to go up into the attic. He said I was welcome to, and that he'd accompany me, only Katie wanted him by her side because she was scared. Rosemary and I therefore went up into the attic with a flashlight loaned to me by Fred. As soon as we entered the topmost room of the old house, we both became aware of a sweet scent. I could see no ghost, but Rosemary said she could. She listened to him tell her about his life, and how it had ended over a century ago. Thomas was from the Victorian era, and had died at the age of 22 from an illness. He was clutching a bouquet of blood-red roses, the medium told me.

"He loved a girl," Rosemary murmured. "He was the secret admirer of a girl. I can see her. She's so beautiful. Oh! No! He's crying."

"Why is he crying?" I asked.

"Because he died before he could reveal his love for the girl. I think her name is Emilie or Emily. There's a trunk in here with the letters he wrote for her," Rosemary said, and looked around.

I scanned the attic with the torch-beam and noticed a large tea chest. Next to the chest was a small trunk. Rosemary opened it and saw bundles of old books and several folded sheets of foolscap-sized paper. There was faded handwriting on these papers, and I brought them downstairs into the light and read them.

They were romantic poems, and one immediately caught my eye. It was entitled: *For Emily* and the verses ran:

> *Beautiful Sweet Emily, will you marry me?*
> *I think I know what your answer shall be.*
> *Emily my love would you have our child?*
> *I suppose you wouldn't consider that wise.*
> *The blue-eyed son I'll never hold,*
> *Our children's bedtime tales – forever untold.*

I eagerly read on, and came to another poem, entitled: *For A Girl I Have Never Met.* It read:

> *I've been crying about a girl, who doesn't even know me yet,*
> *She has autumnal auburn hair, shaded like the sunset.*
> *Her eyes are of a midnight blue, and twinkle like the morning dew.*
> *I'm longing for this friend, but she'll never know how,*
> *She is in the there-and-then, and I'm in the here-and-now.*
> *Someone she will never know, simply wanted to love her so.*

The old books concerned medicine, and on the inside cover of one volume were the faded words of a name. It looked like 'Thomas Pemberton' but the surname was rather too faded to be totally legible. Rosemary had told me that the ghost's surname had been Pembroke. Pemberton was a pretty close match.

When Rosemary came downstairs, she told me that she had persuaded the ghost to go into the next world, where, she promised, his beloved Emily would be waiting to greet him with open arms. The ghost evidently took up the suggestion, because Rosemary said it was no longer about the house. She sensed that the earthbound shade of Thomas had now joined his secret love in eternity. Did the amorous ghost deliver Fred's Valentine to illustrate the fact that it is better to dare to win a heart and fail, rather than spend a lifetime regretting what might have been? Thomas had sadly died without Emily ever knowing about his love for her.

I was most impressed with Rosemary from Bromborough, and I still often ask her to help when I am investigating paranormal goings-on.

## The Haunted Doll's House

In June 2002, Jasmine, a young Prenton girl, received a bundle of gifts for her ninth birthday. Among the presents left in her room, was one that measured two-and-a-half feet by three feet. It was a beautiful doll's house. Jasmine threw her hands to her face in delight as she saw the house, and already a mystery was underway, because the girl's parents could not remember who had given Jasmine that present. Every other gift could be accounted for, except the house – and its contents: two small dolls of a man and a woman that measured about six inches in height. They looked very old and their bodies seemed to be made from a porcelain-like substance. The plain brown paper and string that the house had been wrapped in had no labels attached to indicate who had given the extravagant and unusual gift.

Jasmine's mother, Brenda, telephoned her own mother and asked if she had perhaps given the doll's house as a birthday gift, in addition to the collection of pop CD's she had given Jasmine earlier. Brenda's mother said she knew nothing about it.

Jasmine's father, Eric, inspected the house and saw that it looked quite old. A friend who valued antiques came out to have a look at it and the dolls, and determined that they belonged to the 1860s. He was very surprised at the pristine condition of the gifts, and advised Brenda and Eric to package up the house and its dolls for safekeeping because it was probably worth a pretty penny. Eric saw how much pleasure the doll's house was giving his daughter, and decided he couldn't put it away.

The doll's house was opened by a simple catch that allowed the entire front of the tiny dwelling to swing open. Inside, there were five rooms; the living room, bedroom, nursery and a hallway. The kitchen was accessed through a tiny doorway in the hallway. Jasmine set the house up in the corner of her bedroom, and each night before she went to bed, she would put the dolls in the bedroom of their house, then close the facade quietly before retiring to her own bed.

One night, Jasmine put the dolls to bed before sitting up in her bed to read a magazine by the light of her bedside lamp. A click echoed in the silence. The girl peeped over the magazine – and saw the facade of the doll's house slowly opening. Jasmine stared at the little house for a while, and had a strange feeling that someone was in her room. She felt so uneasy, she slept with the bedside lamp on.

At about ten past eleven, Jasmine was awakened by someone tapping her on the left side of her head. At first, Jasmine thought it was her mother, but when the girl sat up and looked about, she saw that nobody was in the room. All of a sudden a voice whispered: "Jasmine, get up!"

The girl shivered in her bed. Then she looked down to the other side of her duvet. The two dolls had somehow got in beside her. The male doll was shaking, as if throttling the female doll, its tiny hands at her throat. It seemed as if invisible hands were manipulating the dolls, but Jasmine could see no one.

She screamed and ran out of the bedroom. In her panic, she glanced behind and noticed, to her horror, that the dolls were hopping after her. The girl barged into her parent's bedroom in a dreadful state and threw herself on to their bed.

Brenda and Eric tried to reassure their daughter that she had merely had a nightmare, but Jasmine refused to go back into her bedroom. She was in such a state that her father went to investigate and found the dolls lying at the bottom of her bed. He put them back in the house and closed it up.

On the following day, Eric put the doll's house on top of the wardrobe in his own room and later in the evening, he sat on Jasmine's bed and told her once more that she had experienced nothing more than a bad dream the night before.

"Dolls can't come to life, honey," he assured her.

He kissed his daughter, then retired to his own bedroom.

Moments later, Brenda came into the room and told Jasmine a bedtime story. The child dozed off before her mother could end the tale. What Brenda and Eric experienced later that night was related to me via a telephone call I took at the studios of BBC Radio Merseyside.

At around twenty minutes to one in the morning, something wakened Brenda. She opened her eyes and saw the door of her bedroom opening slowly and silently. She expected Jasmine to enter, but she didn't. Suddenly, the doll's house slid sideways off the top of the wardrobe and glided downwards. It halted in mid-air, and at this point, Brenda could hear a child giggling. It sounded like a girl. The levitating doll's house flew slowly through the dark bedroom towards the doorway. Brenda sat up in the bed and decided what she had just witnessed was definitely not a dream. She shook Eric awake and told him what she had just seen. The couple quickly walked along the landing – to find the door of Jasmine's room ajar. Eric switched on the main bedroom light, and found the doll's house back in the corner. What's more, the facade of the house was open and the dolls were missing. Brenda later found them under the duvet in Jasmine's bed.

Enough was enough. Eric tied the doll's house up with string to keep the facade shut, with the dolls secured inside. On the following morning, he drove to the friend who had valued the dolls house and told him that he could have the Victorian collectible and its dolls. He refused to elaborate as to why he was giving it away.

In early July, Jasmine's parents took the girl to see her aunt in Oxton, and during the journey, she suddenly shouted out "Look!"

Her father slowed the car, and Jasmine pointed to an old house. Bizarrely, that house was an exact replica of the haunted doll's house. Eric was so intrigued by the similarity, that he pulled over next to the Victorian dwelling. An old woman wearing a headscarf and a long dark coat walked slowly up towards the gate. Eric was so curious that he got out of the car and approached the woman. He started to tell her about how her home resembled the doll's house his daughter had owned, and wanted to ask if it was possible that the doll's house had been based on her dwelling, but the woman completely ignored him. She simply turned and mysteriously made her way back to the door, entering her house in silence.

Eric considered looking up names of the previous occupants of the old woman's house in the electoral register, but later decided that some dark mysteries are better left unsolved.

## The Face on the Wall

In the year of 1922, Henry Pope, a 70-year-old Birkenhead man, hired 24-year-old Marianne Jones from Wallasey, as a maidservant at his large house on Tollemache Road. Mr Pope had inherited money from his father at an early age, and had wisely invested it in a number of ventures. He married at 35, in 1887, but his wife tragically died a year after the marriage, during childbirth. For the next 35 years the heartbroken Mr Pope remained celibate, to the point of shunning most female company – that was until the arrival of Miss Marianne Jones, who bore a strong facial resemblance to his long-departed wife.

Marianne's application for the post of maidservant was immediately accepted, and the old master of the house was soon making it clear that he had feelings for the young woman. Within the space of a week, Henry and Marianne were enjoying a holiday in Wales, and it was at Snowdon where Mr Pope, with great difficulty, got down on his rheumatoid knee and proposed to Marianne. The unexpected proposal put the young lady's head in a spin, and she looked down at her white-haired employer in confusion, her thoughts in turmoil.

"Will you?" he asked, clutching at her skirt to keep himself steady.

No doubt Miss Jones had thoughts of the fortune she was marrying, and how Mr Pope did not exactly seem to be in the best of health.

"I will," she answered.

A month later the wealthy 70-year-old wed his 24-year-old bride, and Marianne was soon playing the role of Mrs Pope fairly well, even though it was obvious to their servants that she did not love her husband.

Then came the terrible accident.

In the winter of 1923, Marianne's screams reverberated through the house, sending the servants running down to the hallway, where the body of Henry Pope lay with its neck broken at the foot of the last flight of stairs. The corpse, clad in a nightgown, stared lifelessly at the vestibule door, with a strange expression of disappointment.

Two servants examined the body, as Marianne stood in the hallway trembling.

"I'm afraid he's dead," the butler told her, and she promptly fainted.

On the following day, Marianne's brother, Ted, a tall, black-haired man who was said to be a bricklayer, arrived at the house on Tollemache Road and comforted his bereaved sister with a brotherly hug. However, Ted's fondness was subsequently seen to go beyond fraternal affection, when one of the servants barged into the drawing room to find the bricklayer with his face buried in Marianne's cleavage. Marianne was thus forced to admit that Ted was not in fact her brother, but an old romantic acquaintance. The servant was disgusted, thinking it disrespectful to be carrying on in such a way with the lady's late husband barely cold in his coffin.

The Last Will and Testament of Henry Pope was read to the newly-widowed Marianne by a solicitor. The entire house, and its contents, together with Mr Pope's savings, were to be bequeathed to her.

After the funeral, Marianne took Ted upstairs and the couple brazenly made love, much to the consternation of the servants, especially the elderly butler, Mr Robinson, who had been a great friend of Henry Pope. As the sombre silence in the house was invaded by the sounds of the couple's love-making, Mr Robinson packed his belongings and left in disgust, never to return. The middle-aged cook, Catherine Stanton, had pleaded with him to stay.

One morning at 5.30am, Miss Stanton heard faint murmurs coming from upstairs in Marianne's bedroom. The cook crept up the stairs, carefully avoiding the creaky floorboard on the landing. She strained her ears and was rewarded by overhearing a curious piece of information. The widowed Mrs Pope gloated as she told her lover how she had pushed Mr Pope down the stairs. She was explaining that the old man had wanted to use the chamberpot, whereby Marianne had urged him to go to the toilet in the yard, but added that if he felt too old and feeble to make the journey, he should use the pot.

Mr Pope's pride had come before the ensuing fall – when Marianne pushed him from the top step. Miss Stanton experienced palpitations as she heard the dreadful confession, and at nine o'clock that morning she was in the local police station, relating what she had heard to the station sergeant. He told her that there was nothing he could do. The coroner had long decided that Mr Pope's death had been an accident, and the claims of the cook, eavesdropping outside a bedroom in the early hours, would amount to nothing but hearsay. Miss Stanton was very disappointed at the inaction of the police, and she decided she could not live under the same roof as a cold-blooded killer; so she also left Marianne Pope's household, packing her belongings that same day.

Miss Stanton had told the other two servants about the scandalous information she had heard, and although they were shocked, they decided to remain employed at the house for the time being. One of the servants, a Welsh man named David Williams, assured his colleague Edwin Killeen, that God would somehow see that justice was done in relation to the cruel murder of Henry Pope.

Within days, there came a strange twist to this story of the calculating young murderess. Marianne's paramour, Ted, noticed a strange, pink-coloured stain on the bedroom wall where he slept with the widow Pope. It was midnight when Ted first noticed the stain, and he turned up the gas jet to afford a better view. The hairs on the nape of his neck stood on end, and a cold shiver coursed down his spine. The shape on the wall looked like a face; the face of the late Henry Pope.

Ted pointed out the reddish marking to Marianne, who could only see a rusty discolouration, probably caused by fungus or rising damp. However, as the days went by, the stain grew larger, and the image of a familiar face, in profile, could clearly be seen. It was the smiling, life-sized face of the late Mr Henry Pope.

Ted pleaded with Marianne to sell the house and move to Liverpool, but Mrs Pope was convinced that the so-called stain, which she admitted did bear an incredible likeness to her dead husband, had been painted on by one of the servants. Marianne stormed down to the servants' quarters and accused them of perpetrating a ghastly hoax. Messrs Williams and Killeen were baffled by the bizarre accusation. Mr Williams said he was prepared to swear on his beloved Welsh Bible that he had had no hand in any practical joke. The servants threatened to leave because of the false allegation, but Marianne begged them to stay, because she was starting to realise that the stain on her bedroom wall probably had a supernatural origin. Overnight, the face on the wall turned a deep crimson colour, and so alarmed was Ted, that he informed Marianne that he was leaving the house.

"He has come back to haunt you, Marianne, and I want no part in it," cried Ted, as he turned and left her house forever.

The phantom bloodstain on the wall became more vivid until the face was almost of photographic quality. A priest was called to view the strange visage on the wallpaper and advised Marianne to vacate the room while he read several Psalms and sprinkled some holy water about. After the religious ritual, the face remained, only now it started to turn from the profile aspect, until it displayed the full face. David Williams made the sign of the cross when he witnessed the slow metamorphosis.

Enough was enough. Marianne ran pell mell to the police station and hysterically begged to be arrested and imprisoned for pushing her late husband down the stairs. Through a vagary of English Law, Marianne's testimony was not acted upon after a doctor diagnosed that the widow had become mentally unstable as the result of the trauma of bereavement. Marianne got on her knees and pleaded with the doctor to come and see her husband's sneering, accusatory face in the stain on the bedroom wall, but he politely declined the invitation.

Marianne later sold the house, and gave most of her inherited wealth away to various charities. She became a Methodist two years later, and died in Liverpool, in 1955, aged 57.

# The Haunted Photograph Album

In 2002, Betty, a pensioner from Wallasey, telephoned me at Radio Merseyside with a strange and unsettling tale. Betty explained that in October 1999, she was rummaging through a car boot sale in Birkenhead when she came across an old, leather-bound photograph album which contained very old, sepia-toned pictures of people in Victorian clothes. Half of the yellowed pages in the album were blank, but most of the photographs it contained featured two women and a sickly-looking little girl of about six or seven years of age. The two older women looked like a mother and daughter, and the mother's stance and expression always gave the impression of stern severity. To Betty she looked almost wicked.

Betty was intrigued by the old pictures and purchased the album for 50 pence. That's when strange things started to happen.

One morning, Betty came into her living room and found the Victorian album lying open on the table, which was odd, because Betty distinctly remembered putting it away in a cupboard the night before. On the following night Betty fell asleep, and had a terrifying dream. In the dream she was wearing iron callipers on her leg, and was trying to get up a flight of stairs away from a wicked-looking old woman who was dressed in a high-collared blouse. The harsh-looking woman wore her hair in a tight bun on the top of her head, and even in her dream, Betty recognised her. She was the woman featured in the dusty old photograph album. Betty was tormented in her dream as she somehow sensed that the woman was trying to kill her. She was chasing her, coming up the stairs. Betty struggled to escape, but she was having great difficulty climbing the stairs, hampered by the heavy and awkward callipers on her leg. The dream grew even more disturbing when the old woman seized Betty by the throat and started to throttle her.

The pensioner woke up in a sweat and found herself totally paralysed with fear. She listened to the fast, pounding beats of her heart in the darkness of her bedroom. After some time, Betty exerted sufficient willpower to cause her big toe to flex, then slowly regained movement in the rest of her body.

She was so bothered by the disturbing dream that she went downstairs to take another look at the old woman in the album – and got the shock of her life. The album was lying open inside the cupboard, and the page showed a photograph of the sinister old woman. She was smiling up from the faded page. Betty could not for the life of her remember seeing such a picture of the long-dead woman like that in the album before. She slammed the book shut and put it away in a large ornamental biscuit tin.

For the next three nights, Betty had a terrible recurring nightmare, in which she was lying on a bed, unable to move.

In every instance she felt as if she was the young girl in the photo album. For some reason, each time in the harrowing nightmare, Betty saw the shadow of the woman with the bun in her hair sliding across the wall, then her evil grinning face would appear over her. The woman then pushed a pillow over Betty's face, and she could feel the powerful pressure pushing down on her mouth and nose and eyes. Betty would fight for breath at this point, and would end up feeling as though she was suffocating. What made it more unbearable was the paralysis, the inability to move, and the haunting sound of her heart pounding away in her ears. Betty would wake up every time gasping for air, and unable to move a muscle for a while.

Enough was enough. Betty was determined to find out who the people in the photo album were and what the haunting episodes were relating to. She scrutinised the book, and discovered the faint words 'Mary Meer' written on the first page. Betty contacted a friend who was interested in genealogy and tracing family trees, and over a six month period, he pieced together the story of the Meer family, who had lived in the area in the 1890s. What he told Betty shocked and upset her.

Mary Meer had a daughter named Philomena Meer, and a granddaughter named Francesca Meer, who had been a paraplegic. This girl had ended up as a bedridden cripple, and a rumour persisted in the Meer family for years that Mary had killed young Francesca in her bed. The motive for the alleged murder is unknown. Perhaps it was a so-called mercy killing because Francesca was paralysed, and maybe wasn't expected to live much longer. Betty believes the photo album is somehow haunted by the dead Victorian girl's spirit, so she has now given the book of photographs away.

# OTHER TITLES

## Published by The Bluecoat Press

| | | |
|---|---|---|
| HAUNTED LIVERPOOL 1 | Tom Slemen | £5.99 |
| HAUNTED LIVERPOOL 2 | Tom Slemen | £5.99 |
| HAUNTED LIVERPOOL 3 | Tom Slemen | £5.99 |
| HAUNTED LIVERPOOL 4 | Tom Slemen | £5.99 |
| HAUNTED LIVERPOOL 5 | Tom Slemen | £5.99 |
| HAUNTED LIVERPOOL 6 | Tom Slemen | £5.99 |
| HAUNTED LIVERPOOL 7 | Tom Slemen | £5.99 |
| WICKED LIVERPOOL | Tom Slemen | £5.99 |
| MYSTERIES | Tom Slemen | £5.99 |
| MYSTERIOUS WORLD | Tom Slemen | £5.99 |
| A DIFFERENT SKY | Tony Eccles | £5.99 |

HAUNTED LIVERPOOL double cassette audio book, read by Tom Slemen £8.99

Available from all good bookshops
For a free stocklist contact
The Bluecoat Press
45 Bluecoat Chambers, School Lane, Liverpool L1 3BX
Telephone 0151 707 2390

Tom Slemen welcomes details of ghostly experiences and unexplained phenomena. If you have had a paranormal encounter, or a supernatural experience of any sort, please drop a line to:

Thomas Slemen
c/o The Bluecoat Press
45 Bluecoat Chambers
School Lane
Liverpool L1 3BX

All correspondence will be answered.